It Happened In
Delaware

It Happened In
Delaware

Remarkable Events That Shaped History

Judy Colbert

Guilford, Connecticut

Copyright © 2013 by Morris Book Publishing, LLC

Project Editor: Lauren Brancato
Layout: Justin Marciano
Map by Alena Joy Pearce © Morris Book Publishing, LLC

Library of Congress Cataloging-in-Publication Data

Colbert, Judy.
 It happened in Delaware : remarkable events that shaped history / Judy Colbert. — First edition.
    pages cm
 Includes bibliographical references and index.
 ISBN 978-0-7627-6968-1
 1. Delaware—History—Anecdotes. I. Title.
 F164.6.C65 2013
 975.1—dc23

                                        2012044058

Printed in the United States of America

10 9 8 7 6 5 4 3 2 1

This type of book cannot begin to happen without the help, guidance, support, and love from a lot of people. I'm sure I have forgotten a few of you and I apologize. In the meantime, for those I do remember, thank you to:

Nancy Alexander, David Ames, Bill Ayrey, Ted Becker, Elizabeth Boyle, Elaine Brenchley, Hazel Britingham, Dr. Wendy Carey, Dick Carter, Greg Coin, Adele Connelly, Sandra Connor, Dr. Constance Cooper, Kevin Coyle, Bob Cullen, Ray Daiutolo, Michael Davidson, James Diehl, Lorraine Dion, Mike DiPaolo, Marty Emery, Jose Fowski, Michael Francois, Michael Globetti, Liz Griffin, Maria Hess, Mitch Hill, Ann Horsey, John Huber, Melinda Huff, Debra Hughes, Dr. Gordon C. Johnson, Richard Julian, Darren "Digger" Kane, Dr. Willett Kempton, Dave Kenton, Donna A. Knight, David Kraut, Linda Kurtz, Claudia Furnish Leister, Lyn Lewis, Joan W. Lofland, Sudler Lofland, Jenny Lynch, Tina Madanat, Mary Lou Malzone, Aubrey Manzo, Margaret Marcozzi, Governor Jack Markell, Beth Ellen Miller, Jack V. Miller, Molly Murray, Amy Norgate, Linda Parkowski, Gail Pietrzyk, Mike Porch, Chris Portante, Kay Powell, Tony Pratt, Carol Orr, Melanie Rapp, Gary Reich, Jack Richter, Judy Roberts, Beth Rubin, Jim Salmon, Louise Sattler, Frank Shade, Rebecca Shepherd, Dan Shortridge, John Silberstein, David Singleton, John Stanton, Tom Summers, Phillip Sylvester, John Taylor, Nena Todd, James Tomlin, Lisa Tossey, Michael Walfred, Lee Ann Walling, John Werner, Bev Westcott, Tracee Williams, Joanna Wilson, and Dr. Gary Wray.

A special thanks to the Delaware Office of Tourism (and county offices) and all the wonderful people who took the time to assist in my researching It Happened in Delaware.

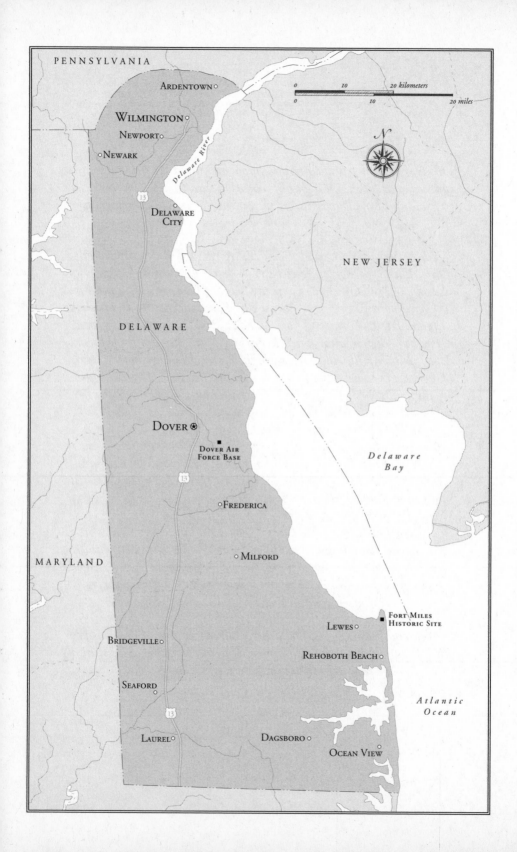

CONTENTS

INTRODUCTION

I love hearing "I didn't know that" when someone reads something I've written. Quite often, I didn't know it until I started researching the subject. That was the case with a number of events related in *It Happened in Delaware*.

Since Delaware is a state that's been around for almost four hundred years, you can reasonably expect that many events and notable people have shaped the history of the state, the country, and even the earth. In some ways, the state has seen drastic changes and in other ways, it hasn't.

You've surely heard or have seen signs that proclaim Delaware the First State—as in the first to sign the US Constitution (December 7, 1787). While that historic chapter isn't included, Caesar Rodney's overnight ride to approve the Declaration of Independence is. It's the first state whose borders were drawn in a semicircular shape (along with Pennsylvania, of course), and the chapter that explains its shape is included.

Delaware had the chance to make history another way—as the final state to approve a woman's right to vote. Unfortunately, they didn't, and they ended up being a footnote to history as Tennessee authorized the constitutional amendment.

Where some people will tell you if life hands you a lemon, make lemonade, in Delaware, when life hands you more chicks than you ordered, make fried chicken. Yes, the chicken industry started as a result of someone taking advantage of a mistake. You'll have a chance to read about the agriculture—from sweet potatoes to frying chickens—that helped shape the state.

You'll also learn that the DuPont laboratories produced the first nylon at the Seaford plant, earning the town the sobriquet of "Nylon Capital of the World." You can also learn about a fiber optic lighting system that is used in museums around the world and that is historic in the way it will help preserve the artifacts of our history.

Education has played an important part in the state's history, first as the birthplace of the Junior Year Abroad program now available in colleges and universities around the world and as part of the Supreme Court case *Oliver Brown et al. v. Board of Education of Topeka et al.* that decided separate but equal was not equal and schools around the country were ordered to desegregate.

A silly idea of "who can throw a pumpkin the farthest" resulted in the annual Punkin Chunkin contest. It's become so well known that it's been featured on cable television and spread to other parts of the country. What's more important is the thousands of dollars that have been raised for scholarships and charities.

What a wonderful combination of yesterday and tomorrow, all in one tiny state. These things make Delaware quaint and modern. Perhaps the thing that will be most surprising to people from other jurisdictions is learning that when people give a phone number for someone I should interview or a place I should explore, they don't include an area code. That's because—as you probably know—the entire state is within the 302 area code.

I hope you have dozens of occasions to think, "I didn't know that."

MIDNIGHT RIDE OF CAESAR RODNEY

1776

If you've seen the movie or the Tony Award–winning musical stage show *1776* about the signing of the Declaration of Independence on July 4, 1776, you "know" that an elderly and decrepit Caesar Rodney rose from his deathbed to make an extraordinary horseback ride through torrential rain to vote Delaware's support of the Declaration.

Except, well, it's the right church but the wrong pew, to cite an old saw. When Sherman Edwards wrote the music and lyrics and Peter Stone penned the book, they took a little literary or theatrical license. The true tale goes something like this.

Great Britain had been involved in what's called the Seven Years War from 1756–1763 (in the Colonies, it was the French and Indian War from 1754–1763). The conflicts stemmed from disputes between the Hanovers (Great Britain) and the Bourbons (France and Spain).

The years at war had depleted the British coffers and they now had to replenish the treasury. This was done with a series of tax acts imposed upon the Colonies. When the Stamp Act of 1765 was enacted, it was the fourth such levy imposed by Parliament. It called for all printed documents (newspapers, wills, insurance policies, lawyers' licenses, leases, liquor permits, school diplomas, contracts, and even playing cards) to have a tax stamp that ranged from a half-penny to ten pounds.

Apparently, Parliament thought the Colonists would be delighted to pay a tax that funded the military protection of Great Britain. Unfortunately, the Colonists didn't think they needed this protection.

The Colonists weren't too thrilled with the idea of the Parliament across the ocean dictating how life should be lived in the Colonies, particularly when they didn't have any representation or voice in Parliamentary proceedings.

In 1767, Parliament added the Townshend Revenue Act, named after Charles Townshend, Chancellor of the Exchequer (treasurer). That little measure put a tax on all sorts of items imported from Great Britain, including glass, paper, paint, lead, and tea. The last straw was the Tea Act of 1773. Agreeing to these taxes was more difficult to swallow than the tea because it gave tacit approval to Parliament to rule and to impose these taxes.

Tea parties in Boston, Massachusetts, on December 16, 1773, and in Chestertown, Maryland, in May 1774, resulted in the sinking of many bales and bundles of tea in the Boston Harbor in the first incident and a virtual tea dunking in the Chester River in the latter. The British retaliated by closing the Boston port. The rebellion in Boston is considered the start of the uprising that led to the American Revolution.

Following the tea dumping, the Colonists established their own governing body with representatives from each colony. Three men represented Delaware: Thomas McKean, George Read, and Caesar Rodney.

Thomas McKean (1734–1817) was admitted to the bar in 1755 and was appointed deputy attorney general of Sussex County in 1756. He would hold numerous political positions, serving in the general assembly of the lower counties, a judge of the Court of Common Pleas, and customs collector at New Castle. He would go on to serve as president of Delaware, chief justice of Pennsylvania, and governor of Pennsylvania.

During his time with the Stamp Act Congress of 1765, McKean proposed that each colony, regardless of its population or size, have one vote, a precedent that was followed in subsequent meetings and eventually to the US Senate with its two senators per state representation. McKean was charged with drafting the Delaware constitution, which was adopted on September 20, 1776.

As the momentum moved toward declaring independence, McKean sided with those who felt it was time to break away from Great Britain.

George Read (1733–1798), the oldest son of a wealthy Irish family from Maryland, was admitted to the bar at the tender age of nineteen, having already finished law school, and within a decade he was appointed to the position of Delaware Attorney General. In turn, that led to his election to the Continental Congress and then to the US Constitutional Convention of 1787. Like most of the population of Sussex and Kent Counties, he supported a movement toward reconciliation with Great Britain. True, he opposed the taxes but felt protests would accomplish the reversal of these measures. Many businesspeople had thriving trade with the British and were reluctant to sever those ties.

Caesar Rodney (1728–1784) was the third member of the Delaware delegation. He, too, was an attorney, living in Kent County, east of Dover. He was elected sheriff in 1755—an extremely important and powerful position—and then was appointed to a succession of other political offices, including the Continental Congress from 1774–1776. Like McKean, Rodney was in favor of independence.

According to Dr. Constance Cooper, head curator at the Delaware Historical Society, the residents and business owners of the Delaware Colony were affected by the taxes as much as those who lived in other colonies. The populace was fairly evenly split on the idea of independence; however, there was one overlying factor that probably had more influence than anything else: Delaware's size. It was so small that the Colonists realized they had to go along with the majority. It wouldn't do if they were the only colony that opposed when the other colonies around them approved the matter. Cooper says that Read, who was not totally opposed to the idea of revolution, felt that they "weren't quite ready and it was not quite time to take this action."

The Continental Congress, having been in session since 1774, was meeting in Philadelphia, and on June 30, 1776, the representatives of the thirteen colonies were presented with a motion for independence. Of the fifty-six representatives, fourteen were from the New England colonies and twenty-one each from the mid-Atlantic and Southern colonies. Of those, forty-eight were born in the colonies and eight were born elsewhere.

Nine colonies voted in favor of the Declaration of Independence, two voted against, and New York abstained. Delaware, with three delegates, was deadlocked because Rodney had returned to Delaware, (where he was the brigadier general of the state militia) to squash a Loyalist riot.

One decision the Congress had agreed to was the conclusion that the vote had to be unanimous for they figured England would see a split vote as a sign of weakness.

When McKean saw the Delaware vote placing the Declaration in jeopardy, he sent a message to Rodney that he was needed back in

Philadelphia. That's when Rodney took off on the eighty-mile ride from Dover. History indicates that at least part of the ride through the pouring rain of a summer thunderstorm, along mucky roads, and through overflowing streams was via carriage and by horseback. The fourteen-hour ride, which today would take about ninety minutes with good traffic, found him at the entrance to Independence Hall on July 2 in time to vote to have Delaware agree to the provisions in the Declaration. That was the deciding factor, and Georgia, the Carolinas, and then Pennsylvania agreed. New York would also join the unanimous vote.

The Declaration was adopted on July 4 and signatures were affixed on August 2, including Read's.

Rodney died in 1784. Although his vote was unpopular with many Loyalist residents in lower Delaware, his participation in our country's history was recognized for his effort and its effect on our destiny. You can see tributes to him throughout the state, for there's a Rodney School District, a Rodney half-marathon, a high school, an institute, an equestrian statue of him, called "Night Rider," in Wilmington, and Rodney's ride is on the 1999 commemorative quarter.

Additionally, just as Paul Revere has a poem dedicated to his midnight ride, Rodney has a poem "Caesar Rodney's Ride" by an unidentified admirer. It begins:

> *In that soft mid-land where the breezes bear*
> *The North and South on the genial air,*
> *Through the county of Kent on affairs of State,*
> *Rode Caesar Rodney, the delegate.*

It continues for fourteen more quatrains, detailing a ride the poet probably couldn't have known in such detail, but fully heralding the triumphant deed.

DOWN BY THE OLD MILL STREAM

1785

When you start wandering along the state's more active waterways, you may see traces of mills, hives of activity nestled along babbling waterways dropping one hundred feet or more from the mountains to their final splash into the Delaware River to the Atlantic Ocean. Over the years Delaware has been home to gunpowder mills (du Pont) and grist and flour mills, logical because we needed to defend ourselves and provide nourishment. A visit to Greenbank Mills & Philips Farm, west of Wilmington (greenbankmill.org), will let you explore the history of the gristmill, the Madison Factory textile mill, and life from 1790–1830. The mill, started around 1677, fell on hard times after the Revolutionary War and was auctioned to Robert Philips in 1790. Philips eventually contacted inventor Oliver Evans (1755–1819), and that's where the story of this mill and milling in general intertwine.

The earliest record of a watermill is from twenty-three centuries ago in Greece. They spread throughout Europe and were modified according to the water supply that ranged from rivers to large tidal surges. The use of waterwheels also traveled to Asia and the Far East. Eventually, as this same population explored and settled this country, they employed the use of watermills, particularly in the New England and Mid-Atlantic areas where the mills powered our industrial revolution.

Of the mills used here, there are three main types, the names of which describe how the wheel is powered. The undershot has the wheel in the water flow, which pushes the wheel upward and forward. It is slightly inefficient because when the wheel enters the water, it blocks the flow. The overshot, which came later, pours the water onto the top of the wheel, pushing it forward and downward. The third, breast-shot, is about midway between the first two, with the water hitting and filling the buckets about the midpoint on the back of the wheel and pushing it downward. As the designs progressed, the mills along rivers and streams had a sluice or built waterway that diverted and controlled the water flow. It could be closed when repair work had to be done on the sluice or the wheel. Occasionally, a dam was built upstream of the mill to further control the amount of water that ran downstream. With enough water and waterpower, mills could be built sequentially so the same water could power numerous mills along the stream or river.

Refinements were made here and there, depending on what the mill was processing, but it would take Oliver Evans, of Newport, Delaware (New Castle County), to truly revolutionize milling. His inventing days started in 1777 when he was twenty-two years old and designed a machine with teeth that would card wool (take clumps or knots of wool and straighten or align it) so it could be processed. About the same time, he also created a new high-pressure steam engine, the first steam-powered land vehicle, for which he was eventually granted a patent in 1789. After the turn of the century, he developed a steam-driven machine that dredged and cleaned the city docks of Philadelphia. He designed a refrigeration machine in 1805 although Jacob Perkins obtained the first patent for a refrigerator.

It was Evans's 1785 invention of the first fully automatic flour-milling machinery for which he is best known. His machinery used bucket elevators, screw conveyors, conveyor belts, Archimedean screws, and something called a hopper boy to spread, cool, and dry the grain. The system involved five machines that handled the grain or meal from the first part of the mill when the grain was emptied from the bag on the ground floor, raised to the top by the conveyor belt powered by the water mill, and then gravity fed into other machines that cleaned, dried, ground, spread, and cooled it until it came out the other end as flour. Once the machines were set in motion and the grain was in the system, no human manual labor was involved. Previously, each step required one or more men, and the Evans flour-milling machine cut that workload down to one man for the entire process.

The first such mill was built on Red Clay Creek, in northern Delaware, followed by many other mills using his system. Other mills along the Brandywine Valley were converted to this more efficient system. The Brandywine Creek comes to a fall line slightly north of Wilmington, and the elevation drops nearly 160 feet, providing a lot of waterpower, which allowed the use of milling machinery long before steam-powered equipment was available. Before the turn of the nineteenth century, twelve mills had been established and they were capable of grinding four hundred thousand bushels of grain a year. Toll roads were built that connected the farms in Lancaster, Kennett, and Concord Pike to the valley. With the direct connection down the Delaware River to the Bay, the flour could be loaded into ocean-going ships.

The Quakers who had settled along the valley were involved in farming and milling and formed a cooperative to produce Brandywine Superfine flour. As early as the beginning of the nineteenth century, their flour was sold along the Atlantic coast and as far away as the West Indies.

The Conestoga wagon, also known as the prairie schooner, was built to haul grain from the Conestoga Valley in the Lancaster County, Pennsylvania, area to the Brandywine flour mills. The wagon could hold several tons of grain. Farther south, Baltimore emerged as the largest city in the South, primarily based on the flour trade due to Evans' milling machinery. Mills along the Jones and Gwynn Falls produced vast quantities of flour and iron ore.

Because a mill could now be operated by one person, the system was installed in some mills that are part of well-known and still existing properties. This includes the one at Mount Vernon, George Washington's home on the Virginia side of the Potomac River. Washington had the system installed in 1791. Sugar Loaf Farm in southwest Virginia used Evans's design when it was constructed in the early nineteenth century. The Newlin Mill complex in southeastern Pennsylvania was built with Evans's design in 1704, operating until 1941, and is used to grind cornmeal today as part of the historic park.

The design was incorporated into mills as far south as North Carolina, as in the Yates Mill, which was built in 1756. Now part of the Historic Yates Mill County Park, outside of Raleigh, it is still used periodically. The machinery necessary for the automated flour mill was adopted by other mills and then it was incorporated into breweries.

It's easy to see how Evans's process revolutionized grain milling. It's also credited, though, as the parent of the assembly line used in automobile manufacturing and other production line facilities.

It would also be adopted for use with taking grain from ships and other bulk carriers and loading it into a grain elevator and then a silo. Previously, this was done by manual labor that could take up to a week to unload a single boat, truly increasing productivity throughout the country, making the United States the industrial leader of the world.

WAS THERE A MULE NAMED SAL HERE?

1829

When you think of canals, you may naturally think of the Erie Canal that opened transportation across the northern portion of New York and connected Albany to Buffalo. Or you may think of the Panama Canal with its six locks allowing ships to travel between the Pacific and Atlantic Oceans. This route eliminates more than eight thousand miles of time-consuming and potentially dangerous sea travel through the Strait of Magellan off Cape Horn at the southernmost tip of South America. If you're new to Delaware or just visiting, you may not even know there's a canal here or that some refer to a place as above or below the canal.

Compared to the Erie and Panama Canals, the Chesapeake and Delaware Canal is a tiny stream. Nevertheless, it has had a major impact on local shipping. The fourteen-mile waterway eliminates about three hundred miles a ship would have to navigate down the Atlantic coast of Delaware, Maryland, and Virginia (the Delmarva Peninsula) and then back up the Chesapeake Bay to arrive at the

Port of Baltimore. That's a lot of time and labor saved with just one waterway.

Thoughts of a canal for this area were first expressed in the mid-1600s by Augustine Herman, a Dutch envoy and mapmaker. More than a century passed before the first surveys were made, and then it was nearly another half-century before the first construction attempt was made in 1804. That plan called for a canal with fourteen locks that connected the Christiana River in Delaware to the Elk River in Maryland. Money, disagreements, and wars conspired (no, not a conspiracy theory) to thwart these plans.

During the first decade of the nineteenth century, nearly six thousand ships traveling between New England and Baltimore met with an unfortunate fate that cost twenty-two hundred lives and more than forty million dollars in property damage. Although most of those accidents were farther north, at least ten lives were lost each year in the stretch between Cape Henlopen in Delaware and Cape Charles at the Virginia end of the Delmarva Peninsula.

A modified canal plan called for four locks and a route from Newbold's Landing Harbor (now Delaware City, Delaware) westward to the Back Creek Branch of the Elk River in Maryland. The four locks were at Delaware City and St. Georges in Delaware and two at Chesapeake City in Maryland. Hand-dug, with picks and shovels, by about twenty-six hundred Irish immigrants, the most difficult part was a sixty-foot rise in elevation in the middle of the state. However, the marshy land was also a problem with frequent dirt slides eroding or filling in what the workmen had just dug.

Finally, in 1829, four years after the Erie Canal opened and almost a century before the Panama Canal opened, the C&D was ready for business. Mule and horse teams led the cargo and passenger boats along the waterway. However, every time a higher lock at Chesapeake City on the western end opened and emptied into a lower lock, that water was lost. This loss was compounded by lock and canal bank leakage and normal evaporation. A steam-operated pump was installed in 1837 to raise the water and then a large waterwheel was added in 1852. A second steam engine was added in 1854, with the two pumps using eight tons of coal each day. The pumps continued in operation until 1927 when the canal was deepened (and widened) by the US Army Corps of Engineers. With a constant depth of twelve feet, the canal became a sea-level waterway, eliminating the need for the locks. (The original pump house in Chesapeake City is now a canal museum that's open to the public.)

Although it would prove its worth in time, money, and lives saved many times over, it was during the Civil War that it showed its value as a military strategy. The War might have had a different outcome except that Union soldiers were loaded onto all the ships in the Philadelphia area in 1861 and sent, through the canal and then the Chesapeake Bay, to defend Washington, DC, from Confederate troops.

By 1938, the waterway had been widened to two hundred and fifty feet and deepened to twenty-seven feet. Its current size is four hundred and fifty feet wide and forty feet deep, which allows two-way traffic except when two passing ships would have a combined beam of one hundred and ninety feet.

Although there have been discussions about deepening the canal and the northern Chesapeake Bay to forty-five feet to take the newer, larger ships, environmental concerns seem to have put those thoughts onto a very back burner. Additionally, as ships have become larger and carry more cargo into Baltimore, fewer ships are using the port. The total tonnage doesn't seem to have changed, but how it gets there has. About 40 percent of the Baltimore cargo ship traffic comes through the canal while the rest comes from the south via the Chesapeake Bay.

The canal goes under five highways and tracks of the Pennsylvania Railroad, and each configuration change had an impact on more than just the canal. It takes about six minutes for the train bridge to be lifted (or lowered) to an initial clearance of 133 feet above mean high water and a second lift of another five feet. Many more ships travel the canal than trains along the tracks, so the bridge is left open for ships. It is lowered or closed when a train needs to cross the canal, about six times a day.

Besides being an efficient boating shortcut, the canal is also listed on the National Register of Historic Places, and it is designated as a National Historic Civil Engineering and Mechanical Engineering landmark.

Where mules and horses once guided the ships, today's traffic is coordinated through state-of-the-art fiber-optic and microwave links. Dispatchers use closed-circuit television and radio systems to safely monitor and move traffic from one end to the other. When foreign ships use the canal, a pilot from the Delaware River and Bay or Maryland pilots' association steers them through the waterway, changing pilots at the state line with the Maryland pilot continuing the trip to Baltimore or Annapolis. For domestic flag ships, a US Coast Guard certified pilot can control the helm. Boat traffic is constant, stopping only in extreme weather conditions. The severely cold winters of 1965, 1978, and 1979 caused the canal to ice over and jam.

By some reports, this old canal is said to be the third busiest canal in the world while others say it's the third busiest in this country. James Tomlin, resident engineer, Chesapeake and Delaware Canal, Army Corps of Engineers, says an average of eight thousand vessels go through the canal every year. That's commercial tugboats, barges, and ships. Some of the freighters leave Japan, stop at the West Coast, go through the Panama Canal, stop at Baltimore, go through the

C & D canal, then up to New York, Europe, the Mediterranean, the Suez Canal, and then back to Japan, picking up and unloading freight at each port. These ships carry millions of tons of cargo to and from the Port of Baltimore and points all over the globe. Tomlin says they do not begin to count the number of pleasure boats that take the canal shortcut on their way from Canada and New England to the Intracoastal Waterway and other points in warmer waters during the winter and back north for the summer.

THAT'S A LOT OF FRIENDSHIP

1899

Delaware is considered a business-friendly state. You can see just how friendly—in numbers—at the end of this article.

The state legislature adopted the Delaware General Corporation Law in 1899, starting the business-friendly trend; it changed the way governmental bodies treated corporations and has had a profound effect on corporate law in the state and throughout the country.

Among other stipulations, the Delaware law allows corporations to shelter their directors from personal liability, protects shareholders from corporate debts, and grants shareholders the right to change the bylaws. Because there is a ceiling to the liability applied to the company directors and officers, the amount and cost of liability insurance provided for each director is lower than for companies incorporated in other states. Also, the statute allows corporations to indemnify directors, officers, and employees, a measure that has been copied in other jurisdictions. It also started a flood of companies coming to the First State for the incorporation process. They may choose to locate their company headquarters elsewhere, but there is someone representing the company physically in the state. In addition to providing a lot of jobs, these corporations, in a simplified cause and effect, are the reason you don't pay state sales tax.

Basically, the law states that Delaware thinks stockholders should determine how their corporation should be governed. The state does not try to tell a corporation how to act or behave. If anything, the state is against regulation. With their effort toward simplification, they eliminate nuances and possible misunderstanding of a section of the code.

Therefore, even in cases heard in other jurisdictions, attorneys in those jurisdictions seek advice from Delaware lawyers because they believe the court in their jurisdiction will follow Delaware law.

Whether or not that attorney will like the answer, at least he or she knows an answer will almost certainly be found within the body of case law in the Delaware court.

Very few lawsuits are brought against Delaware-registered corporations. However, the attorneys involved in the cases that are filed are aware that the judges are the most knowledgeable jurists in the country on the subject of corporations. Plaintiffs and defendants are confident that they will be heard with fairness and by erudite judges.

The state legislature works to uphold the business-friendly reputation and to find ways to reduce business expenses as evidenced by their implementing the cutting-edge practice of electronic signatures. And the office of the Secretary of State thinks and acts more like a corporation than a bureaucracy. The office is staffed through two shifts—working until midnight—to handle requests for expedited services of one-hour, two-hour, same-day, or twenty-four-hour service (for appropriate additional fees) for urgent and time-sensitive filings and making it convenient for people in other time zones to access or deliver information or filings. The agency is also unusual in that it makes a profit.

Support comes from the state's populace, which recognizes the positive financial impact derived from the massive numbers of corporations and generally supports and enjoys Delaware's reputation for solid business decisions.

"Because the laws have been on the books for so long, legal interpretations have been tested on virtually every line of the corporation code," says David Singleton, associate vice president for facilities, University of Delaware. "Nevada's laws are almost a carbon copy of the legislation on the books here. The big difference," he says, "is it sounds better to say you're a Delaware company than a Nevada company." Other states could copy Delaware's legislation, and some have to some extent, but by now they'd be reinventing the wheel.

"Lawyers can tell you how the courts will treat almost any issue that might come up," says Singleton. Additionally, numerous books have been written about the code and the issues brought to the courts so there is a wealth of information sources to research before an attorney has to be contacted.

Working on the old saw that good things come in small packages, Delaware's size, or lack of it, adds to this symbiotic relationship. Everyone knows everyone else and they have to work together, often on a day-to-day basis whether it's a matter of law or civic duty. If two people don't work regularly with each other, they surely know and work with someone in common.

In modified legalese, the state has a Court of Chancery that has jurisdiction over equity cases, and most of them deal with corporate disputes, particularly when it relates to equity and mergers and acquisitions. They do not deal with criminal and tort cases so they are not bogged down with what can be an interminable process. The cases are heard by a judge, not a jury, thus eliminating that time-consuming process. The cases before the Court of Chancery are litigated expeditiously and effectively. Judges have been and still are asked to explain the reasoning for their decision, in writing, thus they have a constantly expanding legislative background and trail for future issues.

During the two hundred years of the Court's existence, they have amassed an enormous body of case law that protects corporations and helps them form the framework in creating new corporations. The Court and the members of the Delaware Bar are considered to be the most sophisticated experts in the subject in the country. Domestic and foreign law students, attorneys, and judges study these cases. Because so many attorneys study Delaware corporate law in school, regardless of which law school they attend or where they practice law, they have a common language all based on the Delaware General Corporation Law.

The result of this increasing number of incorporations is they provide about 26 percent (several hundred million dollars) of the state's general fund. In turn, they help keep down taxes and create a lot of jobs, particularly in the area of forming corporations, which calls for a lot of attorneys and support staff. Certainly, that could not have been foreseen when the act was passed, but it has become significant on many counts.

A second banking issue that added to Delaware's business reputation was the Financial Center Development Act, signed into law by Governor Pierre Samuel du Pont on February 18, 1981. Singleton says that prior to the 1981 act, "it was nearly impossible for a bank to open offices outside its home state." As banks are incorporated under federal law, this new legislation provided an attractive reason for banks to incorporate here. This changed the economic landscape and opened thousands of jobs through the expansion of the credit card banking industry. It offered tax breaks and eliminated consumer rate restrictions (on credit cards) unlike many states that have usury laws that limit the interest rates that can be imposed. More than a dozen major bank holding companies (including J.P. Morgan, Chase, NBNA America, and Citibank) and eighteen other financial institutions have offices in Wilmington. Before becoming affiliated with the university, Singleton was strategically involved in lobbying for the creation of the act, and he attributes its adoption with the creation of more than 35,000 new financial services jobs in the state.

The federal government changed laws about ten years ago that allows banks to be in more than one political jurisdiction. By that time, though, Delaware had already had fifteen years in the business, and the banks that had formed or created offices here have stayed rather than move to some other state.

As an illustration of how business-friendly the state is, the 2011 population was estimated at 907,135 while a year earlier, the number of active business entities (domestic and offshore) incorporated in the state was over 909,000. Yes, more than one incorporated entity per person. Specifically, more than 50 percent of the publicly traded corporations, 63 percent of the Fortune 500 companies, and 60 percent of the companies listed on the New York Stock Exchange and NASDAQ are incorporated here.

The state experienced a 20 percent growth in the number of companies being incorporated here in the first three months of 2011, realizing "seventeen consecutive months of growth since the national economic recovery began in late 2009," according to a report from the Delaware Secretary of State. Additionally, "76 percent of all new US Initial Public Offerings were incorporated" in the state, including the LinkedIn social network site, Gordmans Department Store chain, and Internet radio company Pandora Media. The number of limited liability companies, limited partnerships, and statutory trusts in Delaware continues to grow. When adding these figures together, they're talking about almost a million businesses calling Delaware their home. That's a lot of friends.

ARDEN YOU GLAD YOU LIVE HERE?

1900

When you're playing a game of Monopoly, with its emphasis on property ownership and development, a luxury tax and a utility tax, you're studying the opposite of the economic theory espoused by activist and journalist Henry George (1839–1897), a native of Philadelphia. He advocated a single-tax philosophy. George thought an income tax was counterproductive to initiative and hard work and that only land should be taxed. Some of his followers went on to establish towns from Alabama to Australia, including locations in Hong Kong, Singapore, South Africa, South Korea, Taiwan, and, for our purposes especially, in the state of Delaware.

Shortly after George's death, a few friends and followers from Philadelphia, including Frank Stephens, a sculptor, and Will Price, an architect, used George's economic philosophy to create a utopian community. With financial help from Joseph Fels, a soap manufacturer, they combined George's single-tax philosophy with William Morris's arts and crafts movement (which advocated a return to village life) to create what is the modern-day Ardens.

Just north of the bustling city of Wilmington, three communities were formed. The wooden retreat reminded many of the woods in Shakespeare's *As You Like It* so the name of Arden was adopted for the area. The town of Arden was created in 1900 and now has nearly five hundred residents; Ardentown was created in 1922 and has about three hundred residents, and Ardencroft was established in 1950 and has not quite three hundred residents. Together, they encompass about three hundred acres.

The concept includes letting much of the land stay in a forested condition with paths carved among the trees for all to enjoy. At first, the artists, musicians, theater people, and social activists used Arden as their summer home with the father or husband spending weekends away from the big cities of Philadelphia and New York. Stages at the Arden Club and the New Candlelight Dinner Theatre provided places for performing arts. The visual arts and other activities are held at the Buzz Ware Village Center and are presented by the Arden Club, and the area's many gilds (a variant of guild) help maintain this summer camp feeling throughout the year. By 1922, one hundred people called Arden their full-time home. Ardenites emphasize personal involvement and family participation in events and activities scheduled throughout the year.

The viability and popularity of the single-tax system waned within the first three decades of the twentieth century, but the Ardens survive.

This commonality of thought doesn't mean you'll find the *Stepford Wives* there. Indeed, from the beginning there has been individuality and individual rebellion. Today's residents would consider themselves liberal, tolerant, and environmentalists.

One resident, George Brown, a philosopher and anarchist, became upset over some issue for which he thought he was treated or mistreated, and decided that revenge would be sweet. As a resident, he swore out arrest warrants for violation of the then-strenuous and perhaps onerous Blue Laws that among other things prohibited selling ice cream or playing tennis, baseball, or golf. His citation included the author Upton Sinclair, an Arden resident. Sinclair, who was playing tennis, and ten other residents were punished by having to spend eighteen hours in the workhouse. Sinclair vowed he would, in turn, file an arrest warrant for anyone playing golf or other games on Sunday.

Other prominent people who called Arden home were Harry Kemp, known as the Vagabond Poet; Ella Reeve Bloor, a founder of the Communist party in America; Scott Nearing, American radical economist, educator, writer, political activist, and advocate of simple living; artist Buzz Ware; and Russell W. Peterson (a Republican), who later became governor of Delaware.

More than one hundred years later, the Ardens uphold their single-tax way of life. An individual resident owns the individual home, mostly of Tudor and Elizabethan architecture, and has a ninety-nine-year lease on the land, which can be renewed for another ninety-nine years. All the residents own all the land in common. Each is a member of the community and has a share in the planning and maintenance of the community. Half the land is wooded and open space. Most of the residents still are performing and creative artists and many of the activities throughout the community relate to theater, music, folk dancing, gardening, culinary delights, and other inventive pursuits.

Every year the Shakespeare Gild presents a Spring Show in the outdoor Frank Stevens Memorial Theatre, and every September, scores of volunteers gather to produce the extremely well-attended Arden Fair, a showcase of the three villages and the talented residents. The fair includes live music, food and drinks, arts and crafts, children's games, a used book sale, exhibitions, demonstrations, and more.

Arden, placed on the National Register of Historic Places in 1973, is noted as the only nonreligious utopian enclave to be in existence for more than a century.

To some degree, the rest of the country and parts of the world are coming around to the Georgists' way of thinking that we are the stewards of our land. Today's residents—many of whom live in homes where their parents and grandparents lived—are likely to participate in weed-n-walk tasks (removing ivy, Norway maples, and other invasive plants from Sherwood Forest), or they may help create paths through the recently acquired five-acre parcel adjacent to Sherwood Forest. The five-acre lot had been owned by Marsha Avery since some time in the 1970s and she had planned to develop it as a day-care center and then decided to subdivide the woods and build eighteen homes. New Castle County officials agreed to the plan in 1986. Arden residents tried to buy the site but couldn't handle the $1.8 million price tag.

Fortunately, the project was delayed and the county permit expired. Finally, Arden received a grant that would pay experts to explore the land's flora and fauna. Biologist-consultant Jim White (associate director of the Delaware Nature Society) found the carnivorous insect called the harvester butterfly (*Feniseca tarquinius*), whose larvae eat aphids that eat beech and alder trees. It was the first sighting of these butterflies in Delaware. Botanist Bill McAvoy (Delaware Natural Heritage Program) found the leafy liverwort, also not previously found in the state. These findings were deemed "environmentally significant," so the Ardens' forest preservation effort suddenly had some solid credentials. Former governor Russell W. Peterson (past president of the National Audubon Society and a former Arden resident) supported the preservation efforts.

Due to the Ardens philosophy that the space is available to the public, they received grants toward the new price for Avery's land of $850,000. If the Ardens would pay a third and settlement costs, the state and county would each chip in a third. Henry George would be pleased.

A LITTLE LONG IN THE TOOTH

1900

Dentistry isn't a popular topic unless one's discussing how much the price of dental work has increased over the years and how very little dental coverage is included with most medical insurance policies.

You've surely heard the false legend that George Washington's mouth was full of uncomfortable wooden teeth, but the concept of less-than-perfect dentures was pretty accurate.

By the 1800s, dentists were filling teeth instead of pulling them and using weird materials. Sometimes Spanish and Mexican coins or other metals were pulverized and mixed with mercury. Yes, mercury in our teeth goes back that far. Unfortunately, and as one could expect, the fillings were subjected to hot and cold foods and beverages and outer temperatures and they'd shrink and expand. Eventually, they'd fall out.

Time passed, and then in 1877, Dr. Leaven D. Caulk founded the L.D. Caulk Company. A dentist in Camden, Delaware, Dr. Caulk decided it was time to improve the materials used for fillings. He and a nearby Dover dentist, Dr. Layton Grier, became friends, and when Dr. Caulk died unexpectedly in a horse riding accident, Mrs. Caulk asked Grier and his brother Frank, also a dentist, to assume control of the Caulk Company. Layton ran the business while Frank created new products. By 1898, they had developed a different alloy and new cement to make sure the fillings stayed in place. Besides staying put, thus eliminating constant replacements, they were more comfortable and became popular and successful. This nearly revolutionary development changed the industry and was the first development that brought about the materials that go into your cavities and stay there.

When the brothers Grier moved their business in 1900, they selected Milford as their base of operations. They continued their research into oral disease, eventually introducing synthetic porcelain for filling cavities in the anterior teeth (upper and lower incisors and cuspids) in 1911. Their reputation spread throughout the country and beyond.

The Griers would go on to create the first alloys, composite resins, and later a single component bonding agent, and new impression materials (that stuff the dentist sticks in your mouth to make a mold when you have a crown or replacement tooth in your future). Other inventions include Kadon, the first plastic filling material; Dycal, the first self-cure cap for exposures of the pulp; and Nuva, the first light-cured sealant and filling material. An amalgam they created for use as a dental filling probably had mercury, silver, tin, copper, and perhaps some other trace materials. The materials were easy to acquire, inexpensive, easy to use, and durable. Of course, the use of mercury was questioned and controversial for more than a century and has been phased out of dental use in some countries and most likely will be in other countries within the next few years.

Profit was not the only reason for the company's existence, and their presence was felt in numerous international and local enterprises. The Caulk Company donated dental supplies to the Byrd Antarctic Expeditions of 1928–1930 and 1933–1935, and in return, in December 1934, Admiral Richard E. Byrd named a prominent mountain, Mount Grier, in his honor and as a sign of appreciation for the company's participation in the exploration project. Mount Grier is on the east side of Scott Glacier.

Another interest was the national pastime of baseball. Milford has been home for a number of baseball farm teams, including the New York Giants and the Boston Red Sox, as part of the Eastern Shore Baseball League. This Class D league played off and on in various towns along the Eastern Shore from the 1920s to the 1940s. In 1923 it was the Milford Sandpipers; from 1938 to 1941, it was the Milford Giants; and from 1946 to 1948, it was the Milford Red Sox. Chris Short, a pitcher for the Philadelphia Phillies of the 1960s, is a native of Milford, but that was a lot later.

Dentistry and baseball would combine in the 1920s with Cornelius McGillicuddy Sr. (Connie Mack), a baseball player in earlier years who became the manager of the Philadelphia Athletics baseball team from 1901–1950, longer than any other manager in Major League Baseball history. During his tenure, he became the first manager to win three World Series titles.

Mack and Dr. Walter Grier, another brother, were good friends, and while Grier was attending a Phillies game he asked why Gordon Stanley "Mickey" Cochrane, the star center fielder, was not on the day's roster. Mack explained that Cochrane was out of commission due to an abscessed tooth. Grier offered their dental services, and once Cochrane was back in the lineup, Grier and Mack arranged a mutually agreeable deal. The Griers would provide free dental services to the Phillies and Mack would bring the team to Milford for exhibition games. The Grier brothers were on the board of the Milford Emergency Hospital, and the proceeds from these games were donated to purchase emergency room equipment for the hospital.

Caulk is now a division of DENTSPLY International (dental supply), the world's largest professional dental products manufacturer.

✓ CHRISTMAS SEALS

1907

Most Americans don't remember when tuberculosis (TB, short for tubercle bacillus) was a dreaded disease that had a 50 percent mortality rate. TB killed more people annually than international hostilities and famines. It was and is spread primarily when an actively infected person coughs, sneezes, or even speaks or sings. As the disease is associated with overcrowded and malnourished populations, it's easy to understand how it spreads so easily and thoroughly.

The disease causes a persistent cough—often with bloody phlegm—and chest pain, fever, fatigue, and appetite and weight loss. The disease may spread to other organs and parts of the body. Before vaccines and cures, the only treatment was long stays in relative isolation in sanatoria, many of which were little more than glorified jail cells.

Although a vaccine was developed in 1906, it wasn't until after World War II that it was used in the United States. The combination of the endemic incidence in poorer populations, the high death rate, and the long and expensive cost of care and recovery made funding of sanatoria a project worth tackling. The question was how.

In 1903 Einar Holboell, a postmaster in Copenhagen, Denmark, created stamps (with the approval of King Christian IX and the postmaster general) that would be placed on mail in addition to the regular postage stamp. The funds raised through the sale assisted children who had tuberculosis. The first seals featured the image of Denmark's Queen Louise of Hesse-Kassel and were placed on mail during the winter holiday season, thus becoming Christmas Seals. More than four million were sold that first year, and that raised enough funds to build two hospitals. It also prompted the public to become involved in helping fight a frightfully contagious disease that resulted in seriously infecting one out of every ten people exposed to the disease.

Emily P. Bissell (1861–1948), a lifelong resident of Wilmington, Delaware, came from an important family that valued volunteerism. She helped create the first public kindergarten school, the West End Reading Room (1889), and classes for new immigrants while championing many other civic causes. Yes, this is the same Emily Bissell who would later become active in the anti-suffrage campaign.

Bissell had heard about the Danish practice of selling Christmas Seals and when she learned that her cousin, Dr. Joseph Wales, wanted money to fund a tuberculosis hospital on Brandywine Creek for indigent patients, she started a similar campaign in Delaware. In 1907 she hoped to make $300 and instead raised $3,000. The monies were used to buy a farm for the hospital that Wales wanted. As the stamps, sold at the post office for a penny each, were inexpensive, people of all financial levels could assist, if only buying one stamp. By the second year, Howard Pyle (1853–1911), a noted illustrator from Delaware who was part of the Brandywine School of illustrators and artists, designed the stamp. This fund-raising campaign, which had spread well beyond the Wilmington area, was even more successful, raising more than $100,000.

Little did she know what results would come from her early efforts.

The program caught the attention of the National Association for the Study and Prevention of Tuberculosis, which eventually endorsed and assumed responsibility for the annual campaign. The organization would become the American Lung Association in 1973.

In 1908 Canadians adopted the program in Toronto and Hamilton to help fund local sanatoria. The former *Toronto Globe* newspaper ran front page daily accounts of the campaign's progress, whether it was local or had taken place in some other part of the country. Within a year, more than $6,000 was raised in Toronto and more than $1,200 was raised in Hamilton. Each campaign served two purposes: to help fund recuperative programs and to raise awareness that the disease did not have to be fatal. By 1927, a national program was established that combined to form a single fund-raising effort.

(A similar but unrelated stamp program was established in 1934 to help raise funds for the National Society for Crippled Children— which had been formed in 1919—by selling seals around Easter time. This was during the Depression when the rate of charitable donations had fallen drastically. Today, the Easter Seals organization provides funding for the care of children and adults with autism and other physical and mental disabilities.)

Once a sufficient number of hospitals or sanatoria were built, the monies raised by the stamp sales were used for prevention and education, chest X-rays, and TB testing, thus stopping the disease before it could spread.

Streptomycin was developed in 1943, and the first successful testing of the antibiotic against TB was conducted in 1946–1947, showing that TB could be cured. Unfortunately, some strains of the disease have become antibiotic resistant. It's estimated that there are almost nine million new cases each year with some 1.45 million deaths annually, mostly in developing countries. By comparison, the United States had four cases per 100,000 people in 2007, the United Kingdom had fifteen cases per 100,000, Portugal and Spain had thirty cases, while China had ninety-eight cases per 100,000.

The American Lung Association raises monies now to help treat the sick in developing countries where there are serious HIV/AIDS infection rates (tuberculosis is the leading cause of death among that population) and other populations with immunocompromised conditions (including those taking immunosuppressant medications). Infants and seniors are also more susceptible to catching the disease. Prevention is primarily through a vaccine in infancy and isolation of patients with the disease.

TB diagnosis was difficult because it took a series of procedures and sometimes several weeks for a positive identification. Suspected patients were subjected to chest X-rays, a physical examination, a medical history, and a tuberculin skin test that can show false positive even if the person has been immunized or was exposed to the disease even if it happened decades earlier. Newer tests have been developed and are being tested that show results much more quickly, from ninety minutes to under four hours.

Bissell continued to participate and spearhead the fight against tuberculosis for the rest of her life. Her impact can still be seen today with the Emily P. Bissell Hospital facility in Wilmington, which provides long-term care in 102 beds on a fifty-acre campus. Among other objectives, they specialize in treating patients with respiratory and infectious conditions.

A DAY AND A VOTE SHORT

1920

Delaware makes a big to-do about being the first state to ratify the Federal Constitution on December 7, 1787. What isn't mentioned too often is the fact that the legislature was given the opportunity to be the thirty-sixth state to approve and thereby pass the Nineteenth Amendment to the Constitution that would grant women the right to vote.

Thoughts of and petitions for legalizing women's rights started in Delaware (and elsewhere) shortly after the Civil War with the passage of the Thirteenth Amendment that eliminated slavery, the Fourteenth Amendment that granted citizenship to everyone born in the country, and the Fifteenth Amendment that guaranteed men the right to vote, regardless of race. Seriously, could women's rights be far behind? Well, yes, although in the 1870s, married women in Delaware were given the right to own property, make wills, and control their own earnings.

The issue heated up a little toward the turn of the twentieth century when the Delaware Equal Suffrage Association was established. The group was affiliated with a similar national organization, the one established by Susan B. Anthony and Elizabeth Cady Stanton. The battle heated up in 1913 with rallies and parades throughout the villages and small towns. It was to no avail as the state denied women the right to vote.

The Delaware suffragettes joined with others, looking southwest about one hundred miles to Washington, DC, to petition Congress to amend the US Constitution. In fair weather and foul, women joined together and picketed and heckled elected officials when they had public speaking engagements, questioning how long women had to wait until they could vote. Just as today, they protested in front of the White House and across Pennsylvania Avenue in Lafayette Park.

Back in Wilmington on May 2, 1914, thousands of people stood and cheered (and possibly some jeered) as hundreds of people—men and women, adults and children, white and black—paraded and rode in cars and on floats in support of the amendment.

Those in favor said if they were good enough to work in the factories while men went to war to fight for our freedom and rights, they should be good enough to have the right to vote. Those opposed said men should take care of the voting box because if women were involved in voting they couldn't campaign for causes without being suspected of having an ulterior motive.

The campaign ramped up even more in 1917, although there were some who felt the women were unpatriotic because they caused a distraction in the daily operation of the states and country. The pro-suffragettes picketed the White House during the cold of winter on into the gloriousness that is Washington in the spring (the famous cherry trees had been planted around the Tidal Basin and other areas of Washington in 1912, so they would have been in full bloom during part of the months-long campaign).

By June, the situation had become tense, and the police started arresting some of the picketers for obstructing traffic. The picketers questioned why they would be arrested and charged now when they hadn't been in previous months. Those arrested were given a choice of paying a fine or going to jail. Among the Delaware women who were incarcerated were Mabel Vernon, Annie Amiel, and Florence Bayard Hilles. Amiel would be arrested several times and spend more than one hundred days in jail. When some of the women resorted to hunger strikes and the prison guards had to force-feed them, the popular opinion of their actions turned in favor of the picketers and eventually the arrests stopped.

The effectiveness of the prison terms was powerful, but not as a deterrent. It's said that women who had been put in jail went out across the country to speak in favor of voting rights, wearing their prison uniforms.

President Woodrow Wilson finally changed his public opinion and asked Congress to pass the Susan B. Anthony Suffrage Amendment. Finally, in June 1919, with Delaware Rep. Caleb R. Layton (R) and Sen. L. Heisler Ball (R) voting in favor and Sen. Josiah O. Wolcott (D) voting against, the amendment was approved.

Now it was up to the legislatures of three-fourths of the forty-eight states to approve the amendment. The procedure went smoothly enough, and within ten months thirty-five states had ratified the amendment. From the remaining states, Delaware seemed the most likely to approve the measure and become the thirty-sixth and final state necessary for its passage. Delaware Governor John G. Townsend Jr. (R) favored the action and his general assembly also was Republican. As the legislature sat and discussed the measure, from March to June 1920, the country's eyes were on Dover.

Florence Bayard Hilles of the National Women's Party and Mabel Lloyd Ridgely of the Delaware Equal Suffrage Association (which would become the League of Women Voters) led the suffragettes. On the other side were Mary Wilson Thompson and Emily Bissell, the woman who had shot to celebrity status a decade before when she started the Christmas Seal campaign to fight tuberculosis. All of the women leaders on both sides were involved in numerous charities and civic causes. Their passion for and against suffrage was earnest and heartfelt.

Those in favor wore yellow flowers and those against wore red ones. It has been referred to as the American version of the War of the Roses.

The upper house approved the measure by a vote of eleven to six on May 5 and turned the measure to the lower house. The campaigning and lobbying were fierce. One reason given to vote against was the thought that if women were allowed to vote, they'd support a national vote for Prohibition. As the house session came to a close, they had not brought the matter to a vote, which probably would have lost if it had been on the agendum.

A few months later, by a margin of one vote, the Tennessee legislature approved the measure and became the thirty-sixth state to ratify the amendment. Women's suffrage became part of the US Constitution in August 1920.

Instead of being at the forefront, again, Delaware missed out on making history when it came to women's suffrage.

GOOD THINGS COME IN SMALL PACKAGES

1921

Delaware is the second smallest state; only Rhode Island is smaller. And although it was the first state to ratify the Declaration of Independence, it was probably the last state to have its borders absolutely defined.

Pennsylvania is on its north; the Delaware River, Delaware Bay, New Jersey, and the Atlantic Ocean on its east; and Maryland is on its south and west. And, just to confuse things a little, there's also a piece of the state that's on the eastern side of the Delaware River in what is otherwise known as New Jersey. The borders follow physical features (the river, bay, and ocean) and man-made lines so the border is straight, irregular, and curved. Delaware and Pennsylvania are the only states with curved borders.

As with most boundary disputes at the time the Colonies and states were established, the arguments dealt with access to navigable water that would reach, in this case, the Atlantic Ocean. They also involved which jurisdiction had more land under its governance.

More land also meant more landowners, which meant more taxes to the state government. Unlike Europe, this was a new country (except to the Native American tribes of the Delaware, also known as Lenni-Lenape and the Susquehanna), and there were no land claims dating back generations and centuries. Boundaries had to be established by scientific methods.

Disputes arose between the Calverts of Maryland and the Penns of Pennsylvania and had been discussed numerous times for more than three generations. English kings had granted land to each family, but the deeds weren't precise and sometimes overlapped. In 1763 a British astronomer, Charles Mason, and a surveyor, Jeremiah Dixon, were hired to survey what would eventually be called the Mason-Dixon Line. The best-known part of that line, today, is between Maryland and Pennsylvania. Looking at the date, it's easy to see that the Mason-Dixon Line was not drawn to separate north from south because the line was surveyed a century before the Civil War took place. The idea of a boundary delineating slave from non-slave states didn't arise until the Mason-Dixon Line was mentioned in Congress when they were debating the Missouri Compromise in 1820.

The easiest place to start unraveling the complex issue of Delaware borders is the southern border that divides the state from the lower portion of the Delmarva Peninsula, which belongs to Maryland and Virginia. This east-west line, known as the Transpeninsular Line, was first surveyed in 1751 by John Watson and William Parsons of Pennsylvania and John Emory and Thomas Jones of Maryland. It runs from the Atlantic Ocean for about thirty-five miles or the halfway point to the Chesapeake Bay. North of that line is Delaware although at the time they were considered the "lower three counties" of Pennsylvania. Mason and Dixon would confirm these measurements in the 1760s, but they started on the northward measurement.

Survey work started about five miles west of the town of Delmar (on the Delaware–Maryland border) at a place called Middle Point (the middle of the Transpeninsular Line) and went north for eighty-three miles, just north of Newark. Stones were placed every mile and eighty-one of the original stones and six replacements mark their survey.

Once you leave that line, things become a little more complicated. The northern boundary between Delaware and Pennsylvania was established as an arc extending twelve miles from the New Castle County courthouse cupola. It's often referred to as the Twelve-Mile Circle. It zigs and zags to the low-tide mark of the Delaware River, onto the New Jersey shore. Then, it picks up the rest of the southern sweep of the arc, after which it follows the middle of the main river channel of the Delaware.

A group of Swiss, Finns, and Dutch had settled the land first, in what is now Wilmington, in 1638, with Peter Minuit as its leader (and then Peter Stuyvesant). A second colony was established in 1651 at what is now New Castle, and they eventually took over the original settlement. The land went back and forth until it was transferred to William Penn in 1682. He wanted direct access to the ocean, requesting the western border of the Delaware River, and in the process acquired the three lower counties. Although it might sound logical that the smaller three counties would want to be rid of the larger representation, the Pennsylvania landowners became upset with decisions that had to be approved by the lower counties and the general assembly split into two bodies in 1704.

One of the original problems was one piece of land with almost as many names as there were drops of water. What is now Cape Henlopen was variously called False Cape, Cape James, Cape Cornelius, Cape Hinlopen, and Cape Inlopen, and then there was a question of just where the cape was located. One source said it was down by Fenwick while most of the others said it was north by Lewes.

A major complication arose in the charter for Pennsylvania that was processed in 1681. It gave William Penn the land west of the Delaware River and north of the 40th parallel. It excluded, however, only land within the Twelve-Mile Circle.

In the nothwestern part of the state is a wedge-shaped piece of land, west of the Maryland–Delaware curve (in the northwestern part of the state), that measures about eight hundred acres. Pennsylvania claimed it even though Delaware governed. Both states appointed a committee in 1889 to determine where it belonged. They decided it was Delaware's.

Finally, a decision was made that any land beyond the western reach of the north-south line but within the Twelve-Mile Circle would belong to Delaware. Eventually it was decided that Maryland didn't have any claim to the wedge, and until Pennsylvania and Delaware separated, it belonged to the Penns. This discussion and additional surveys continued until 1921, when both states agreed that the wedge belonged to Delaware. Pennsylvania ratified the finding in 1897, but Delaware was a little slower, waiting until 1921. The US Congress also approved it the same year. Phew.

HERE A CHICK, THERE A CHICK

1923

Delaware carries the "Blue Hen State" nickname because the Delaware Revolutionary War soldiers took Blue Hen cocks with them for entertainment between battles and skirmishes.

So it shouldn't be surprising that chickens rule the roost in Sussex County. It's a trend that's been going on for more than eighty years. It was a strange twist of the wishbone, however, that caused the broiler industry to be here in the first place.

According to James Diehl, media relations manager for Southern Delaware Tourism and author of *Remembering Sussex County (DE): From Zwaanendael to King Charles,* you have to go back to 1923 when Mrs. Wilmer (Cecile) Steele, part of a farming family in Ocean View, ordered fifty chicks to replace laying hens that had aged out of their usefulness. Due to a misplaced zero, she received five hundred instead.

Rather than return them, the Steeles built welcoming accommodations and raised the chicks for meat instead of eggs. The broiler industry was hatched. Five hundred chickens became an order for a thousand chickens the next year, ten thousand the following year, and by 1927, they were raising twenty-five thousand chirping, feathered fowls.

That first broiler house has been preserved at the University of Delaware Agricultural Experiment Station near Georgetown.

The neighbors saw a good thing, and soon there were several hundred poultry farms in the county. Of course, chickens aren't the only factor in the industry. Others earn a living by selling building materials, chicken feed, and related supplies.

For a while a chicken breed called the Delaware was popular in the state. It was established around 1940 when George Ellis, another Ocean View resident, developed a new fast-maturing breed with a pleasant temperament that produced good meat and were good layers (large- to jumbo-size brown eggs). He originally called them "Indian Rivers" in honor of his hatchery and the local river. He eventually changed the name to Delaware. It remained an important part of the chicken meat industry until the even faster-growing Cornish Rock was introduced into the breeding stock in the 1950s. Alas, the Delaware stock has dwindled to the point of being "threatened," with fewer than a thousand breeding birds in the country. On the positive side, local farmers are reintroducing the meaty and tasty breed and are hoping it will regain some of its popularity.

By 1948, a trade association, the Delmarva Poultry Industry, Inc., had been organized and they, in turn, created the Delmarva Chicken Festival that was held in Georgetown. Today, the festival rotates among the three states and attracts about 20,000 people. The festival, free to attendees, has educational displays, pony rides, music and entertainment, games and carnival rides, home and trade shows, arts and crafts exhibits, and chicken prepared in just about every way you can imagine. Don't expect to find any other meat—from corn dogs to burgers—at this festival. It's all chickens.

Wander around the grounds and you'll learn that it's been illegal since the 1950s to feed hormones to commercially raised chickens and that nearly 1,700 farm families raise broiler chickens on the Delmarva Peninsula. You can see local chefs presenting cooking demonstrations (samples available) and watch baby chickens hatching.

Among the highlights is the world-famous ten-foot-diameter frying pan produced in 1950 by the Mumford Sheet Metal Company, Selbyville. It's said to be the largest (at least, one of the largest) frying pan in the country. Three tons of golden fried chicken (about 800 quarters) can be cooked at one time in the 650-pound pan with an eight-foot handle. It uses 180 gallons of oil at a time. Apparently, no one's measured how far the appetizing aromas that waft off the pan travel to lure hungry passersby into the festival.

According to Diehl, "There are more broilers—young chickens (under thirteen weeks old) suitable for broiling—produced in Delaware's southernmost county than in any other county in the United States; in fact, the race isn't even all that close. Sussex County poultry companies produce nearly twice as many broilers per year as Cullman County, Alabama, the country's second largest producer." The hens that lay the eggs that produce broilers are eventually sold as older, tougher, stewing chickens. A hen generally produces three hundred eggs a year. The males that aren't used for breeding are sent off to be food for falcons and other birds of prey.

According to the Delmarva Poultry Industry, Inc., approximately 73 percent of Delaware's cash farm income was from broilers in 2009.

Although Sussex may be the number one chicken-producing county, Delaware is not the number one state. Georgia produced the most chickens in 2010, with 1,313,500. Arkansas, Alabama, and North Carolina came in next. Delaware is eighth. In all, the country produced 8,625,200,000 (that's billion with a *b*) broilers in 2010, weighing nearly 50 billion pounds. That's a little more than $730,000,000 in total bird value raised in 2009. Most of the grain grown in Delaware is used for chicken feed. According to Georgetown, Delaware, Mayor Brian Pettyjohn and Jim Smith, president of Delmarva Poultry Industry's board of directors, 250 trucks leave chicken processing plants across the peninsula on a daily basis carrying nine million pounds of poultry.

Townsends, Inc., Allen Family Farm, and Mountaire Farms of Delmarva, three of the country's top broiler-producing companies, are headquartered in the county. Perdue Farms, Inc., has its offices in nearby Salisbury, Maryland. That means more than eight thousand people—or nearly 12 percent of the county's workforce—is employed in the poultry business.

From a century ago when chicken was served as a Sunday or special occasion meal, Americans now consume about eighty pounds per capita every year. That figure is expected to grow to ninety pounds per capita per year by the end of the decade. Chicken sales account for about 40 percent of our meat market, with beef second at 30 percent and pork third at 24 percent. Annual current per capita consumption of beef is sixty pounds and pork is forty-seven pounds.

The United States is the world's largest poultry producer. While chicken has been touted as a healthier product than red meat, it's also considerably less expensive, an important factor in the economy of the late 2010s. Almost half of the chickens grown in this country are purchased by consumers for at-home use. Another 40 percent went to restaurants, particularly the fast food industry that sells nuggets, strips, sandwiches, and full or half chickens. The rest is sold overseas (Canada, Mexico, Central America, Caribbean, Sweden, United Kingdom, Japan, and the Middle East) or used in pet food.

A BROADENING EXPERIENCE

1923

Taking off for faraway places for some additional education can be credited historically to the first brave explorers of a thousand or more years ago who stayed awhile to pick up a foreign language. International travel stalled during the Middle Ages and then picked up again in the sixteenth century. Two hundred years later, visiting professors started teaching in schools in other countries. And then a formal program for students going abroad for a semester or more was started at Indiana University in the 1870s.

Following World War I, several groups—educational, religious, and nonviolent—within the United States started exploring ways to broaden their students' outlook and approach to the rest of the world. They focused on international exchanges and, with the guidance of Nobel Peace Prize winners Nicholas Murray Butler and Stephen Duggen, formed the Institute of International Education in 1919 (IIE), which eventually would become the Council on International Educational Exchange (CIEE).

Just as Delaware was the first to sign the Constitution, the University of Delaware at Newark became the first to initiate a foreign education program into its curriculum. A half-century after Indiana's experiment in foreign study, UD French Professor Raymond W. Kirkbride, University of Delaware at Newark, proposed that several of his students spend a semester in Paris studying at the Sorbonne. (This was and is still known as the Latin Quarter because students who had been attending the school since it was founded in the mid-thirteenth century came from various countries and spoke a variety of languages, but all of them had a command of Latin that allowed them to bridge their different native tongues.)

Kirkbride was a World War I veteran who had seen the devastation caused by the war and by the lack of understanding and communications among nations. While fighting in France, he met and talked with the locals and realized that cross-cultural relations could benefit people who crossed international borders to learn about the culture and beliefs of other people and countries. From there the knowledge would be distributed to the circle of business associates, friends, and others who had contact with the people who had participated in the exchange.

Suggesting such a global education program took nerve and bravery because the United States was in a firm isolationist frame of mind. Most might have considered the idea to be ridiculous. Nevertheless, Kirkbride received approval from Walter S. Hullihen, the university president, but not from the university itself, which meant no funding to send the students overseas. Hullihen realized that the opportunity for better language knowledge and skills would be complemented by a deeper understanding of other cultures, particularly by those who wanted to go into international relations and diplomacy.

The two men sought and received funding from public and private sources, including then-Secretary of Commerce Herbert Hoover and local philanthropist Pierre S. du Pont. The eight juniors—Austin P. Cooley, Francis J. Cummings, David Dougherty, Herbert L. Lank, William K. Mendenhall, J. Cedric Snyder, T. Russell Turner, and J. Winston Walker—and Kirkbride set sail aboard the SS *Rochambeau* on July 7, 1923. They spent six weeks in a crash course in French in Nancy, France, before they set foot in Paris. According to University of Delaware records, the trip was extremely successful and became more international than anticipated when Lank met his future wife, Turner became a basketball superstar, and Turner and Cummings won the Sorbonne's diploma of French civilization, a highly desirable recognition.

From this baby step, UD went on to send students to Switzerland and Germany in addition to France. The Delaware Foreign Study Plan, funded by the school, was ultimately called the Junior Year Abroad program. It was a tremendous success and was soon copied by such schools as Brown University, Columbia, Harvard, Penn State, Princeton, Wellesley College, and Wesleyan University.

Duggen and the IIE took the American students abroad program and reversed it so foreign students could come to the States to study. A new nonimmigrant visa was established with the Immigration Act of 1921. A reciprocal exchange program was established between the States and Czechoslovakia and eventually American students were participating in education programs in Russia, China, and Argentina.

The establishment in 1946 of the Fulbright Program, named for US Sen. J. William Fulbright (D-Ark) has seen more than three hundred thousand students from fifty countries participate in programs in more than 155 countries (as of 2010).

In the twenty-five years after the program started, 902 University of Delaware students have spent their junior years abroad. Then, post–World War II conditions in Europe and a new university president with other priorities caused a hiatus to the UD program as of 1948. Nevertheless, students who had participated in the program continued to have reunions, publish an alumni directory, create a newsletter, and raise monies to buy an ambulance for France during the War.

By 1972, the foreign study program had been reinstituted at UD, although it was a short "winterim" stay between the fall and spring semesters. Students went to London, Paris, Rome, Vienna, Munich, Berlin, Hamburg, and Geneva. Enough students participated that a plane was chartered to hold all the students involved in the program, and Pan Am painted the fuselage with the words "Delaware Clipper."

The program spread to the English department and a full semester's study and became its own department, Overseas Study.

With the initiation of the Benjamin A. Gilman International Scholarship program, part of the International Opportunity Act of 2000, the study abroad program was opened to a more diverse student population and the number of countries where programs are available.

From this small beginning, the program grew nationally to almost 50,000 students by the end of the 1980s to more than 260,000 by the end of the last decade. Other changes have seen the program grow from classes taught in English that lasted a few weeks with students living together to courses that run a semester or two that are taught in the country's language and students living with host families.

This figure represents only about 1 percent of all students in post-secondary education, according to the Institute of International Education's Open Doors report. Most of the more than 260,000 students from the United States head to China, France, Italy, Spain, and the United Kingdom. Lately, students are heading to less traditional countries, particularly outside of Europe, including Argentina, Chile, Peru, and South Korea, with students studying natural history, language, and culture.

Other options added to these programs include US colleges or universities that have a branch campus or campuses abroad, direct exchange programs between American and foreign institutions that offer a "visiting student" status. The student pays the tuition and receives any existing financial aid of his or her college while attending the foreign school and receives academic credit at the American college or university. As of 2006, Goucher College in Baltimore, Maryland, became the first national liberal arts college in the country to require that every student participate in a foreign study program as a graduation requirement. Students can choose from more than three dozen countries from Argentina to Uganda, from intensive, summer, semester, and year-long programs. They offer a voucher of at least $1,200 to help cover travel expenses.

Ninety years after the first foreign studies to France, UD now sends students to all the continents but Antarctica, studying such diverse topics as mechanical engineering, animal science, and business administration.

DELAWARE'S MOTHER ROAD

1924

Wherever you go in Delaware, to paraphrase a child's song, it's "here a du Pont, there a du Pont, everywhere a du Pont." That's the case with T. (Thomas) Coleman du Pont (1863–1930), who was born in Kentucky, received an engineering degree from the Massachusetts Institute of Technology, moved to Johnstown, Pennsylvania, and then, with his cousins Alfred I. and Pierre S. du Pont, bought the family's explosives company and moved to Delaware. After numerous acquisitions and antitrust lawsuits, he sold off his share of the business in 1914.

During his years with the family company, he decided the state needed a paved road running north–south, connecting the three counties from Wilmington to the Maryland state line and from there to the rest of the country. He convinced the legislature that such a road was necessary in 1911, and that he would build it. With the authority to buy right-of-way throughout the state, he started work on what he said would be "a monument a hundred miles high" that would be laid out on the ground.

His idea was to build a highway three hundred feet wide the length of the state that had lanes for vehicles, bikes, horses and carriages, and trolleys, with separate northbound and southbound lanes, and room for trees to line the roadway. Even more important, he promised to pay for the construction and then turn control over to the state.

Prior to this time, the unpaved dirt roads of Kent and Sussex counties were barely passable during inclement weather. The general assembly enacted a regulation calling for all automobiles to have a horn or bell and that they should slow down when nearing a vehicle drawn by an animal. The road conditions seemed deplorable to a man who loved automobiles and found that they were of no use in rainy weather. It was a rich man's game, for only a few hundred cars were even registered in the state.

Despite the boon this would be to Sussex County farmers, they balked at the idea of losing their land, especially because they thought du Pont was building the road for his own personal gains. As a result, du Pont paid up to four times the land's value for many parcels. Besides increasing the price of the road, the negotiations delayed its construction.

In 1916, the US Congress enacted the Federal Highway Act, which provided construction assistance to states with a highway department. A year later, in 1917, a Delaware state highway department had been formed (which would become the Department of Highways and Transportation, and then DelDOT) that had the authority to build and maintain a statewide highway system. The department assumed control of the building of du Pont's road with the agreement from du Pont that he would continue to pay for its construction, at a rate of up to $44,000 a mile.

It would take until 1924 before the first two lanes of the DuPont Highway were complete, but they paved the way to revolutionizing road construction throughout the country. Locally, farmers and merchants in Kent and Sussex could now take their products to markets in the northern part of the state and beyond. They were no longer beholden to the railroad. It would prove invaluable for the chicken industry that had started in 1923 and the sweet potato industry that started in 1925.

His monument, two lanes wide, was completed in July 1924, costing him $3,917,004. In 1933, three years after du Pont's death, the state widened the highway to two lanes each way, divided by a median, between Dover and Wilmington. It was the world's first divided highway, and du Pont's highway would eventually measure in at 96.7 miles. It has been and parts of it still are Route 13 (from Dover to Wilmington), Route 113 (Dover to Delmar), Highway 1 (new construction to relieve some traffic from the original road), DuPont Highway, DuPont Parkway, and Sussex Highway (in Sussex County). Some of it has been replaced by Highway 1 and some of it has been relegated to access road status. It remained the main north–south road until the new controlled-access Route 1 was completed between Wilmington and Dover in 1995.

Seeing the success of this road, the state highway department started paving other roads, and by 1926, nearly six hundred miles were finished with a hard-surfaced road connecting every town and village.

The state led the nation in highway construction by the 1930s. When the general assembly transferred all county roads to the state highway department in 1935, they had nearly twenty-six hundred miles of unpaved roads that would take three decades to pave. As of 2002, when DelDOT celebrated its eighty-fifth anniversary, they were in charge of 11,111 lane miles of roadway and 1,350 bridges.

Following his 1915 retirement from business, du Pont became a member of the Republican National Committee (1908–1930), helping to reunite divergent factions of the party. He served as a Republican in the US Senate during two different terms (1921–1922 and 1925–1928), resigning before his term was completed due to poor health. The monies he provided for the road carrying his name are still the record holder as the biggest personal gift in highway history.

SWEET POTATOES

1925

The sweet, sandy Delaware soil, particularly in Sussex County, was noted as being particularly good for growing sweet potatoes as early as 1868. Rich in calcium, potassium, and vitamins A and C, the sweet potatoes grown in Delaware were said to be sweeter than those grown in other parts of the country. Such varieties as Big Stem, Up-the-River, and Little Stem were all good in sweet potato pie. Nancy Hall, Hayman, and Southern Queen were saved for table eating after baking. They all tolerated the peninsula's sandy soil. Although often confused with yams, which come from Africa and Asia, they are not from the same family. Our sweet potatoes originated in Central and tropical South America, where they were grown as long as five thousand years ago.

In 1925, a state directive suggested Delaware farmers should increase their plantings so they could grow a hundred bushels of sweet potatoes to supply the markets of Philadelphia and New York, rather than just growing a few bushels for their own use. Eventually, the market would go as far as Pittsburgh and Boston.

Farmers followed that advice, planting enough potatoes to average 100,000 bushels a year through the turn of the century, then producing 440,000 bushels a year for the first two decades of the twentieth century. That amounted to about two thousand acres growing fifty bushels an acre. As the number of acres grew to six thousand and the per-acre yield increased to ninety-six bushels, sweet potatoes stayed a primary cash crop until the 1940s. Elsewhere, farmers were seeing only an average of seventy-seven bushels an acre. Potatoes were a labor-intensive crop that started with planting in seed beds in February and then individually transplanting the young plants into the fields when the ground was warm enough.

As the crop became more important, the sweet potato house was developed where potatoes could be stored and dried before they were ready to be sold. The house was two or three stories tall, longer than wide (ranging from seventeen by twenty-three feet to twenty-four by thirty-six feet), with a coal- or wood-burning stove that would keep the house at a constant (twenty-four-hour) temperature of fifty degrees. That meant someone had to keep watch on the stove and stoke it, morning and night, particularly once the first frost had taken place. This went on from October through February.

A central walkway divided deep, three-sided storage bins that ran down either side of the long dimension of the house, but the walls of each bin did not directly abut the walls. Rather, there was about four inches of space between the bin and the exterior wall. The second floor also didn't reach to the walls. Generally, the potatoes were stored on platforms or slats instead of directly on the floor. The doors and any windows were left open to allow air to circulate until the first frost. At that time, the doors and windows were shut and the stove was lit.

Building the bins away from the walls allowed the air and then the heat to circulate throughout the house, drying or curing the potatoes. If one farmer didn't grow enough to need an entire house, one was operated as a cooperative with other farmers renting or owning however many bins were needed to hold a year's crop. Another style of tobacco house had the bins back to back with a walkway between the bins and the outer walls. In other words, there was no central walkway in these houses.

The exterior of the house was unlike any other house or barn in the area. It had at least three layers of siding, and sometimes as many as five, alternating with an application of horizontal boards, then diagonal, vertical, diagonal the other way, and finishing with a horizontal application. Sometimes weatherboard, straw, or insulating paper was used. The windows, usually on the second and third floor, were used to access the upper floors to load and unload the crop. These, too, were tightly insulated.

It's unclear who designed or even conceived the sweet potato houses. The potatoes could not be eaten when first harvested. They had to be dried or the moisture would lead to rot. As it took at least a month for the potatoes to be ready for market, that made them edible in time for Thanksgiving and the winter holidays. However, the potatoes were not all sent to market at one time but were parceled out over a number of months to maintain the price.

Just as peaches (still the state fruit) had been an important crop that died out to disease, the potatoes succumbed to black rot or stem rot, a particularly destructive disease. It started eating away at the crop as early as the 1920s, becoming a more significant factor in the 1930s, and pretty much destroying the crop by 1940. Men going off to World War II reduced the labor pool, which meant labor costs rose. The growth of the chicken industry changed the cultural landscape.

The sweet potato crop moved south, particularly to Georgia, the Carolinas, Alabama, and Texas, although a large crop was produced in Louisiana and Virginia. Southern farmers introduced new varieties that had a much shorter growing season and produced higher yields, thus decreasing the cost of growing potatoes.

By 1900, Delaware was ranked twelfth in the nation in acreage among states producing sweet potatoes, dropping to thirteenth in 1910, fourteenth in 1920, and fifteenth in 1930. Those are astonishing figures considering how small Delaware is. By volume, Delaware's ranking was twenty-third in 1900, seventeenth in 1910, fourteenth in 1920, and then down to twenty-second in 1930. North Carolina is today's leading domestic producer, followed by California, Louisiana, and Mississippi.

A dozen or so sweet potato houses remain as historical reminders of the tuber's heyday. Some of them have had some alterations made so they can be used for today's farming. However, they maintain their tall and narrow shape and are fairly easy to spot as you drive around Sussex County. The Wright, Chipman, and Collins potato houses were added to the US National Register of Historic Places on November 15, 1990. The Wright house is one and a half stories; the Collins is two stories; and the Chipman is two and a half stories tall. Other potato houses named to the list at the same time that are near Laurel are Moore, Phillips, Ralph, Rider, Stanley, Hitch, and Hearn. Two other houses, Dickerson and West, are near Delmar. Maple Leaf Farm potato house is near Hebron.

STRONGER THAN STEEL

1939

While Jerry Siegel and Joe Shuster were busy creating the superhero who could "fly faster than a speeding bullet, [was] more powerful than a locomotive, and able to leap tall buildings in a single bound" in the 1930s, the scientists at E. I. du Pont de Nemours and Company, referred to as DuPont, were working on the first fully synthetic fiber that would be "stronger than steel, fine as a spider's web, more elastic than any of the common natural fibers, and splendidly shiny." According to Dr. Charles M. A. Stine (1882–1954), company vice president and director, the product would be called nylon. Credit was given to Wallace Carothers, a former Harvard instructor who was head of the nylon research team at DuPont.

The creation of nylon was not a serendipitous "aha" moment that stemmed from scientists looking for one thing and finding another. The first evidence of nylon was created in April 1930 when a lab assistant discovered a strong polymer that could be drawn into a fiber. Because it had a low melting point, the scientists went another direction and it wasn't until 1935 that they returned to what would become nylon. Toothbrushes with nylon bristles were the first item of what would become a long list of goods made partially or totally with the synthetic material.

Prior to nylon, we relied upon cotton, wool, linen, and silk for clothing and other fabric needs. Each had its advantages and disadvantages, but silk—particularly for women's stockings—had several drawbacks, including expense and fragility.

Nylon was the first synthetic fiber, made of coal, air, and water. The thread is stronger than steel while being more elastic than natural materials. When heated, it becomes silky shiny. Once DuPont determined that low-cost production was possible, they decided women's stockings would be the first target market. Nylon was introduced to the world at the Golden Gate International exposition in San Francisco/Oakland and the New York World's Fair with its "Dawn of a New Day" theme. Dr. Stine astonished audiences by telling them that DuPont had a factory already producing thigh-high, seamed nylon stockings that felt better than silk, didn't bag, and dried more quickly than silk.

The first nylon stockings were purchased on October 24, 1938, at a Wilmington, Delaware, store. DuPont didn't patent the term nylon with the thought that nylon hose or nylons would replace the previously popular phrase of silk stockings. The new stockings were instantly popular. DuPont built a temporary plant in Wilmington to produce the stockings and then a larger, permanent plant ninety miles away in Seaford, Delaware. It opened on December 12, 1939, and as of the 1970s, more than four thousand employees worked there, around the clock week in and week out. It earned the town the name, "Nylon Capital of the World," but they still couldn't produce enough. To meet the demand, another plant opened in Martinsville, Virginia, in 1941.

The history of nylon hosiery came to a screeching halt once the United States entered World War II and the War Production Board had DuPont convert its nylon manufacturing for such war materials as parachutes, airplane cords, flak and bulletproof vests, and B-29 bomber tires. Once the Japanese captured the Philippine Islands in 1942, where manila was made into rope, DuPont nylon was used to make the lines that secured ships to piers. Only nylon stockings produced before the war could be purchased and then they were usually sold on the black market for exorbitant prices. It wasn't uncommon to have to pay $20 a pair for nylons that had been about $1 in pre-war days.

Once the war with Japan was over in August 1945, DuPont quickly started producing nylon hosiery and newspaper headlines were nearly as bold as those announcing the Japanese surrender. DuPont promised "Nylons by Christmas," which would prove to be overly optimistic. The demand was so much higher than the supply—even with a limit of one or two pairs to a customer—that between August 1945 and March 1946, women lined up outside department stores and caused "nylon riots," akin to today's fight for new shoes and electronic gadgets. Reportedly, forty thousand women lined up outside a Pittsburgh, Pennsylvania, store where only thirteen thousand pairs of stockings were in stock. Newspaper reports told of hair pulling, scratching, and other un-ladylike behavior and noted that no other product had ever received so much free publicity. An estimated sixty-four million pairs of stockings were sold that first year.

According to DuPont records, they started working with another chemical version of nylon in the early 1950s that produced a "bulked continuous filament (BCF) nylon that was tested for six years as the carpeting in the Hotel du Pont in Wilmington. Along with Antron, another nylon, it revolutionized the carpet industry. DuPont is still the world's leading manufacturer of nylon, polymers, and textile fibers."

When you do the math, you realize that 2013 is nylon's seventy-fifth anniversary, and Debra Hughes, curator of collections and exhibits at the Hagley Museum and Library in Wilmington, has been working on a display in honor of that anniversary and the significant impact nylon has had on our lives. Because nylon can have heat-set pleats and creases; resists fading by sunlight; is easy to dye; is resistant to insects, fungi, mold, and mildew; and has a greater elasticity than other fibers, it is used in an incredible variety of products.

As DuPont continued to develop products following their motto of "Better Things for Better Living—Through Chemistry" (which was shortened to "Better Living Through Chemistry" and then abandoned), we now have tents and tarps, ponchos, seatbelts, meat wrappings, sausage sheaths, shower curtains, aprons, tablecloths and placemats, umbrellas, ropes, carpets, musical instrument strings, machine screws, gears, hair combs, and numerous other products that are made totally or partially with nylon. From nylon, DuPont also developed Orlon, Dacron, Lycra, polyester, and other fibers that have revolutionized the fashion industry in particular and other industries in general.

Perhaps because it is not readily biodegradable, some recycling is being done converting the material to reusable pellets. However, even in today's fashion of bare legs, a new demand is being heard for these thigh-high, seamed sexy coverings, particularly in the original packaging, perhaps proving that nylon is stronger than steel.

IN DEFENSE OF OUR COUNTRY

1942

Delaware was and is home to numerous forts (Altena, Casimir, Christina, Delaware, DuPont, Hoarkill, New Amstel, Ogleton, Oplandt, Reynolds, Sekonnessink, Sikeomess, Swanendael, Trefalddighet, Trinity, Union, Whorekill, to name a few) and military camps, with two in particular playing eventful roles in our history and coming to two diametrically different ends.

The Delaware coast—along the Atlantic Ocean, the Delaware Bay, and up the Delaware River—was considered prize territory to protect against enemy attack. Building a fort, it was figured, would help prevent enemy ships entering the bay and river and having access to domestic shipping and the factories, chemical plants, and oil refineries in Wilmington, Philadelphia, and surrounding areas. The newly constructed ships coming out of the Philadelphia shipyards provided plenty of targets.

When the SS *Waukegan* ran into the St. Georges Bridge over the Chesapeake and Delaware Canal in early 1939, the canal was closed into the early part of 1942 until the bridge could be removed and the waterway cleared. This meant ship traffic that would have gone through the canal when transiting between Philadelphia and Baltimore had to sail up and down the Chesapeake Bay and up and down the Atlantic coast, leaving them exposed to the German U-boat fleet.

Fort Saulsbury was the first fort constructed, in 1918. Named for Delaware's US senator, Willard Saulsbury Sr., who served from 1859–1871 and then as the state's attorney general, it's now often called Delaware's Forgotten Fort. Built next to Slaughter Beach, about six miles east of Milford, the fort on about 160 acres was completed almost at the end of World War I. A handful of personnel kept the fort going for the next two decades. The huge and greatly feared German surface fleet never made it to this side of the Atlantic.

The onset of World War II changed the fort's countenance, and in 1940 new buildings were erected. It stayed at the ready until 1942 when Fort Miles was completed on 1,550 acres of land. As Fort Saulsbury was no longer a vital factor in the coastal defenses, it became a prisoner of war camp (along with nine other prisoner camps—particularly Fort Delaware—throughout the state) and as many as three hundred German and Italian military personnel were kept there. While sixteen million of our young men were off fighting the war, Michael Davidson of the Fort Saulsbury Historical Association says many of the prisoners worked at local farms (picking field crops and orchard trees, plowing, etc.) and poultry processing plants. Some worked at the local canneries, including the Libby, McNeil and Libby Cannery in Houston, Delaware, west of Milford, where they canned tomatoes, peas, and beans. The last POWs were removed from Fort Saulsbury on January 11, 1946. It's said that several of them returned to Sussex County because of the pleasant countryside and people they'd encountered while they were here.

Three years after Fort Saulsbury was decommissioned in 1945, it was purchased by the Kendzierski family for $12,700. They, in turn, leased it to the Liebowitz Pickle Company for pickle processing and storage. It was used for other purposes over the years and today is thought to be the only surviving WWI-era fort that is basically unchanged and in private hands. History buffs are requested to view the fort on the FortSaulsbury.org website rather than bother the private owners.

Meanwhile, Fort Miles, a few miles southeast of Fort Saulsbury, at Cape Henlopen, near Lewes, was bigger and could handle larger sixteen-inch guns, each capable of lobbing 2,250-pound shells more than twenty-three miles. Two of Fort Saulsbury's twelve-inch Howitzer guns, with a range of fifteen miles, were moved to the new fort.

Dr. Gary Wray, coauthor of *Fort Miles (DE): Images of America,* says twelve sixty-inch Sperry searchlights with eight hundred million candlepower were erected along the waterfront (ten on the Delaware side and two on the New Jersey side), throwing a twenty-five-mile beam across the bay and out to sea.

Despite the demeaning reputation of the Italian military, according to Wray, the lights were installed to protect against an attack by the Italian navy. Wray says, "They would have a number of merchant ships twenty–thirty miles off the shore protecting fast little motor torpedo boats (like our PT boats), which is how they sank the battleship *Queen Elizabeth* in December 1941."

Another military concern was the German superiority in the field of submarines (the Germans commissioned more than 1,500 subs). Starting in January 1942, the German sub fleet, or wolf pack, had a devastating destroy rate on our ships, many times off the Delaware coast, and killed thousands of sailors. This continued through the spring of 1945 until the German surrender. On May 4, 1945, the German sub U-858 was off the Canadian shore when the captain received word from Germany to surface and surrender. The captain turned the ship toward American waters and surrendered on May 10, off the coast of New Jersey, and was instructed to go to Fort Miles. When the captain surrendered, it was the first time an enemy ship had surrendered to the United States since the War of 1812.

Fort Miles was named for Lt. Gen. Nelson Appleton Miles (1839–1925), commandant of Fort Monroe, Virginia, where former Confederate President Jefferson Davis was held prisoner. Besides the aforementioned big guns, the fort had a variety of other weapons that had a range of 1,300 to 35,300 yards. The still-standing observation towers that were built along the Delaware and New Jersey shorelines extended the effective firepower of the sixteen-inch guns to their full twenty-five miles, much farther than it would have been from just the ground-level line-of-sight or from one tower alone. More than 2,200 men and women were stationed there.

With such defensive power on our side, the Germans took less offensive action near the Atlantic coastline than anticipated, although several of our ships were sunk. One was the USS *Jacob Jones,* which was part of the Neutrality Patrol that tracked enemy wartime movements in the Western Hemisphere. Completed in 1919, decommissioned in 1922, and recommissioned in 1930, the *Jones* (named for Commodore Jones, 1768–1850) was a Wickes class destroyer with a dozen torpedo tubes. It could travel an impressive thirty-five knots an hour. In December 1941, she started escort duty along the Eastern Seaboard until she made contact with a German submarine U-578 off Cape May, New Jersey, in late February 1942. The sub sent two torpedoes into her port side, which severely damaged the *Jones* and she went dead in the water. All but two dozen or so officers and men were killed. Most of the survivors managed to reach lifeboats and put them in the water. However, apparently in anticipation of finding submarines during their patrol, the men had set the depth charges and they exploded as the ship sank, further demolishing the vessel and killing several of the original survivors. A dozen sailors were rescued, one dying on the way to Cape May, and all others were lost at sea.

By the 1960s and 1970s, the US Navy had assumed control of part of Fort Miles, using it as an ultra-secure and covert base for an underwater SOSUS (Sound Surveillance System) listening facility. Microphones were placed strategically along the continental shelf and used to track the Soviet submarine fleet during the Cold War. The navy stopped using this as a SOSUS base in 1996.

As the land was converted from military to public use, the sixteen-inch guns were cut up and sold as scrap. Now, a similar cannon barrel, number 371 off the USS *Missouri* (the ship where the Japanese officially surrendered on September 2, 1945) has been restored and placed at the fort, all sixty-six feet and 120 tons of her.

Having served its defensive purpose and now no longer needed, the land could have become just another beachfront community. Instead, it's now Cape Henlopen State Park. As private as Fort Saulsbury is, that's how public Fort Miles is. As violent as its purpose was, that's how peaceful it is today. You can walk around what remains of the fort, tour the fort museum and grounds, and celebrate the "greatest generation" our country has known and ponder how our fate would be altered if the fort had never existed.

SEPARATE, BUT NOT EQUAL

1954

Although Delaware was north and east of the Mason-Dixon Line (which was established well before the slavery question was being contested), it was one of seventeen states that had legally approved slavery. Particularly in the lower two counties, the economy was based on agriculture, which took a lot of labor that was usually performed by slaves. Quakers and Methodists, however, were opposed to slavery and actively participated in the Underground Railroad. When the Civil War was declared, Delaware refused to secede from the Union. Reliance upon slave labor decreased and many slaves were freed and were productive at many, but not all, levels.

In Delaware, as elsewhere, segregated schooling was proving to be anything but "separate but equal." The 1896 *Plessy v. Ferguson* decision by the US Supreme Court pertained to equal facility of railway passenger cars for whites and blacks. However, the case law was expanded over time to incorporate almost everything that pertained to separate but equal, including school construction to instruction.

By 1950 the city of Wilmington had a population of 110,000 with about 17,000 blacks. Prejudice was not as evident there as it was in other parts of the state even though, between de facto and de jure segregation laws, many public facilities were still segregated. This was about to change with the groundbreaking decisions made in two court cases, *Belton v. Gebhart* and *Bulah v. Gebhart.*

In the early 1950s full integration of the Claymont High School was implemented and that brought to a head any unrest that had been fomenting. One problem was brought to court in two cases and they had nothing to do with whether the education itself was equal. They dealt with the ease with which white students could get to school that was prohibited for black students.

Ethel Louise Belton, a fifteen-year-old, spent two hours a day on a school bus to attend a run-down Howard High School in Wilmington. She also spent time a few afternoons a week (after school) walking to another school for other classes. Howard was the only school in the state that offered business and college preparatory studies for black students, and while it was good at what it did, the spacious and well-maintained white school Belton passed on her way to Howard had courses and extracurricular activities that weren't available at Howard.

Similarly, Shirley Bulah walked more than a mile from her Hockessin home to her school, Hockessin Colored Elementary. Her mother, Sarah, requested that Shirley be able to ride the bus (that went by her home and her school) with the white students or have a bus of her own. The request was denied.

When educational equality was discussed, it was noted that the teachers at the white schools had smaller class sizes and lighter work loads than the teachers at the black schools. Louis L. Redding, of Wilmington, took notice and decided to act.

Redding was a graduate of Harvard University who had become the first African American to practice law in the state and a noted civil rights attorney. His record and accomplishments in civil rights matters earned him an esteemed reputation. He had filed suit against the University of Delaware in 1950 to allow black students to attend the school. He won the case, *Parker v. the University of Delaware,* and the school became the first state undergraduate university desegregated by court order. (Redding would later be the attorney of record in a 1961 case, *Burton v. Wilmington Parking Authority,* also taken to the US Supreme Court, that held that segregated tax-exempt parking accommodations—and specifically the Eagle Coffee Shoppe located within the parking lot that was partially funded by the city of Wilmington—were illegal.)

With attorneys Jack Greenberg, Thurgood Marshall, and others, Redding filed a civil action to correct the inequality on April 1, 1952. He took on the cases for Belton and Bulah, for which he did not charge, according to reports from the National Association for the Advancement of Colored People. Instead, he said the NAACP chapters should raise funds for court costs.

Redding's argument was that segregation went against the Fourteenth Amendment, which guaranteed equal protection under the law and that the segregated school system harmed the black students. If financial support hadn't been provided by the du Pont family, the black schools would have been in worse condition than they were.

Francis B. Gebhart, as head of the State Board of Education, was named in the case. He and the state's attorney general said that the subject should be decided by the US Supreme Court.

Comparing the equality of teachers and opportunities in one school could be and probably was subjective and, theoretically, in some cases one school could be better in one area and the other school be better in another area. Therefore, a large part of the case—with examples and professional testimony—was based on a comparison of insurance valuation for Delaware schools. The colored Hockessin school was valued at $6,250 while the nearby white school was valued at nearly seven times that amount, proving that the facilities were separate but not equal.

The *Belton v. Gebhart* case was heard by the Delaware Court of Chancery in 1952, stating that the US Supreme Court had not declared that schools must be integrated but had ruled that the facilities and opportunities must be "separate but equal." As the black Delaware schools did not fit that description, Seitz declared that the schools should be integrated immediately.

The Delaware cases survived an appeal to the state supreme court. That decision was appealed and the cases were merged with four others, *Briggs v. Elliott* (South Carolina), *Davis v. County School Board of Prince Edward County* (Virginia), *Bolling v. Sharpe* (Washington, DC), and a case from Kansas. The major difference between the Delaware cases and the other cases was the Delaware cases were the only ones that had decided in favor of an integrated school system while the other jurisdictions were focusing on maintaining segregation while improving the "equal" part of the equation. The five cases became *Oliver Brown et al. v. Board of Education of Topeka et al.*

The case was first argued before the Supreme Court on December 9, 1952, reargued on December 8, 1953, and finally decided on May 17, 1954, about the time Claymont's first integrated class was graduating. The final decision from the US Supreme Court ruled that "separate but equal" was not working and should be struck down.

Most of the Delaware schools were willing to abide by the Supreme Court's decision and integrate, except for Milford High School. The local citizens were unhappy about the ruling, so Redding sent a telegram to Governor J. Caleb Boggs asking for National Guard assistance with the school's integration on September 27,

1954. Fortunately, the integration process proceeded smoothly and the military support was not needed.

A life-size statue of Redding with an African-American schoolboy and a white schoolgirl stands in front of the Redding City-County government complex in downtown Wilmington.

ASH WEDNESDAY STORM

In early March 1962, true spring weather was still a few weeks away, and the storm that was forecast for that first week didn't seem to be worthy of any deep concern. This was long before twenty-four-hour cable news stations and weather alerts kept us informed of every increase in wind speed and every inch of rain or snow. It was also before Doppler radar and satellites that watched storms as they marched or danced or idled until they hit land or died.

However, in a true "perfect storm" situation, the low pressure system that was making its way eastward and northward up the coast was blocked in by a fast-moving and then stationary high pressure system. That blockage kept the rain falling and the tides pummeling the shoreline and blocking any draining water from returning to the ocean. Compounding that was the spring equinox, which caused higher than normal tides, and a new moon that brought even higher tides.

Suddenly this nor'easter became the storm of the century, sticking around the Delaware coast for five high tide cycles over three days (most storms last one to two high tides). In all, it killed forty people, injured more than a thousand others, and destroyed property worth millions of dollars in the six states that it swept through. Seven of the fatalities were in Delaware, six from a single family caught in a car trying to escape the rising waters.

North Carolina's Outer Banks and Virginia Beach, Virginia, were the first areas to be slammed by the storm. Then, on Tuesday, March 6, the storm attacked Ocean City, Maryland, before heading up to the Delaware beach towns of Fenwick Island northward to Lewes and towns farther inland on the Christian holiday of Ash Wednesday. Winds were blowing at thirty to forty-five miles an hour with gusts up to seventy miles an hour. Waves were topping out at twenty to thirty feet and where high tides were measured, they reached nearly nine feet in some places. The storm would continue up the coast, leaving devastation along the New Jersey coast (where it ripped away part of Atlantic City's famed Steel Pier) and onward to New York.

On the western side of the Chesapeake Bay, where temperatures were a little lower, snow blanketed the land and disrupted life as snow is wont to do.

The advancing Ash Wednesday storm, which would also be called the Coastal Storm of the Century, the High Five (referring to the number of tides), the Great Nor'easter, the Great Atlantic Storm of the Twentieth Century, and the Storm of '62, approached almost as a wall of water one sees in pictures of tsunamis making landfall. The waters crashed and smashed homes and buildings, making them floating two- and three-story houseboats until the waves dissipated and the buildings were deposited a few miles west of their original location, with some relocation as far as Indian River Bay. Roads were covered with sand, and pieces of boardwalk, buildings, fences, and other structures were picked up and tossed with no sense or order.

The 1960 census counted fewer than 500,000 people in the entire state of Delaware, most of them in the Wilmington area. The Sussex County population didn't even top the 75,000 mark. Seaford was the big hub of activity, primarily because of the DuPont nylon factory located there.

Most residents along the coastline were summer folk who had boarded up their homes the previous Labor Day weekend and weren't expected back until at least Easter or more likely a few days before Memorial Day (still called Decoration Day in 1962) weekend or not even until the weekend itself. They looked forward to opening the front and back door and sweeping out the sand that had seeped through the cracks during the winter. They certainly didn't expect to see the splintered remains of their summer cottages.

Those who were there or didn't think to evacuate had lost power, running water, and sewer service by Thursday. There was no way to drive or walk to safety. In Delaware alone, it's estimated that the storm destroyed 1,923 homes and did $70 million (in 1962 dollars) in damage to public, private, and personal property. That's probably closer to $500 million in today's money. According to Dr. Wendy Carey, Delaware Sea Grant College Program, 923 of the homes were "damaged structurally by wave action."

Delaware is notably flat, and as the waves ebbed and flowed, they ate away whatever dunes existed that protected inland properties. Most of the building damage was caused by the sand erosion. Dr. Carey says, "At the time, many structures were built with foundations that were slab-on-grade or concrete block." The erosion undermined houses and commercial establishments until the shallow foundations fell away and the buildings toppled into the sea. Those that weren't consumed dangled at precipitous angles that made them look like the next wind would be the last. Dolle's candy store went, the fronts of the Atlantic Sands and Henlopen hotels were pulled away, and roads were covered, cutting off access in many places. The first Rehoboth Beach boardwalk was built in 1873, mostly destroyed in a 1903 storm, rebuilt, destroyed again in 1914, rebuilt, and then saw a devastating demise in the 1962 storm.

Even though there was no flood or storm damage insurance at the time, stores, hotels, and other businesses that provided services to summer tourists still had to be up and running by Memorial Day weekend. According to Tony Pratt, administrator for the Delaware Department of Natural Resources and Environmental Control (DNREC)'s Shoreline and Waterway Section, Rehoboth Beach and Bethany both had their boardwalks rebuilt before the start of the summer season.

The storm was a wake-up call for everyone concerned about the shoreline, the environment, and the commercial viability of the area. Some changes would be made almost immediately and some would take awhile. Some lessons are still being learned.

One of the first changes came in 1968, when the federal government created the National Flood Insurance Program (NFIP) that allows property owners in designated flood plain areas, with restrictions, to buy insurance to protect against losses from flooding. Pratt says it's a carrot and stick program where the carrot allows local citizens to be covered and paid following a flooding incident. The stick part calls for the community to enact flood hazard zoning ordinances dictating what types of foundations, venting, and other construction concerns are required or allowed.

Because all coastlines aren't the same, particularly when it comes to bedrock and wetlands areas, there can't be one-size-fits-all regulations. In Sussex County, new construction and modifications are subject to four different inspections. The buildings have to be certified for their storm resistance, including wind loads and wave action. The roofs and attics have to be strapped down so they won't pull off the walls and fly away. Footers and pilings, framing and energy insulation are all considered in the design and construction. Lewes calls for construction that can withstand winds of 120 miles per hour.

If buildings along the Delaware beaches were required to sink footings and foundations to bedrock, says Pratt, they'd have to go down to ten thousand feet. Instead, they use what's called skin friction that considers the weight of the house or building being proposed fully furnished, with people to determine how many pilings are needed and how deep they have to be sunk. So, a house may have pilings that are seventeen or eighteen feet into the ground with a ten-foot clearance above the normal beach level. This allows flood waters to come inland and not undermine the footings and buildings.

Builders were no longer allowed to bulldoze sand dunes because they "blocked the view of the ocean." Other requirements call for planting such vegetation as Cape American Beach grasses to prevent wind erosion of the dunes and promote dune growth (by catching windblown sand and by roots that help secure the dune that exists) and fencing the dunes so people won't walk over them. Native Delaware plants can be purchased at local nurseries and garden shops.

In 1972, the state legislature enacted the Beach Preservation Act that defines the beach area as running from mean high water line of the Atlantic Ocean and the Delaware Bay seaward 2,500 feet and landward 1,000 feet and from the Delaware/Maryland line at Fenwick Island to the Old Marina Canal north of Pickering Beach. A building line—which parallels the coastline—demarks where construction is prohibited seaward of the line without a Coastal Construction Permit.

In honor of the fiftieth anniversary of the storm, a "Delaware Coastal Vulnerability and Sustainability—1962–2062" workshop was held in March 2012 that reviewed the past, present, and future storm preparedness and reviewed a documentary film about the storm of '62. Work still has to be done. Fortunately, although the "super storm" Sandy of late October 2012 disrupted life and forced many to evacuate the beach area, the main Delaware damage was to the sand dunes and not the buildings and boardwalks. Of the more than 100 United States deaths attributed to the storm, no lives were claimed in Delaware.

CAPE MAY–LEWES FERRY

1964

Thoughts of a way to connect the seventeen miles between Cape May, New Jersey, and Lewes, Delaware, probably were considered as early as the nineteenth century when steamships would periodically transport people between the two states across the Delaware River. Ferries between the two states and between New Jersey and Pennsylvania were a frequent sight. However, any permanent solutions suggested to the connection problem sank like leaky boats in bad weather. Many saw a need, but not a way to fulfill that need.

On September 19, 1935, the Wilmington-Deepwater Tunnel Company proposed a $10 million tunnel that would run under the river, at about the location of the Delaware Memorial Bridge. They showed that nearly 665,000 vehicles used ferries to connect between Wilmington and Penns Gove, New Jersey, and they anticipated that more than a million vehicles would use the tunnel annually. The tunnel toll would be considerably less than the cost of the ferry ride, they said. Alas, the project did not receive approval.

When the Garden State Parkway was completed in 1957, providing a limited-access highway from the metropolitan populations in the New York and Philadelphia areas to the resorts along the Atlantic Ocean, including Cape May, it was considered a highway to nowhere.

New Jersey legislators and private companies made several attempts to start ferry service that would connect the GSP to areas south and west of the Delaware River, but it wasn't until 1962 when New Jersey, Delaware, and the US Congress created the Delaware River and Bay Authority (DRBA) that any progress was made. A 1956 feasibility study was updated and the Cape May–Lewes Ferry was established in 1963. The Delaware elected officials wanted a second span to parallel the Delaware Memorial Bridge (the original span opened on August 16, 1951), and the New Jersey folks wanted their ferry, says Mike DiPaolo, executive director of the Lewes Historical Society. Each would finally get what they wanted.

Two other events dovetailed to make the ferry feasible. First, as the DRBA was establishing their ferry, the Cape Charles–Little Creek Ferry in Virginia was ceasing operation with the April 16, 1964, opening of the Chesapeake Bay Bridge–Tunnel. Four (of the seven) then-obsolete Virginia ferries were acquired by the DRBA: the SS *Pocahontas,* SS *Princess Anne,* SS *Delmarva,* and the MV *Virginia Beach.* They were rechristened and became the SS *Delaware,* SS *New Jersey,* SS *Cape May,* and the MV *Cape Henlopen.* The Authority also hired the former general manager and four of their ferry captains.

The second event was the 1963 collapse of the massive menhaden fishing industry, says DiPaolo. "The fish stock was so depleted that it came to a screeching halt. The local economy [of Lewes] was almost wholly dependent upon the little fish. It brought in guys who rented houses, repaired boats, kept the grocery stores busy to feed the crews, and provided business for bars and nightclubs. Hundreds, if not thousands, of men kept the town stable and prosperous economically." Fortuitously, the ferry came along and provided the jobs that kept the kids in the area instead of leaving for life in a big city. "It was very exciting." Today, as many as one hundred people are employed by the ferry during the off-season and three hundred during peak season.

Ferry service started on July 1, 1964, complete with a week's worth of celebrations, boat races, a jet plane squadron flyover, parades with prizes for the best floats, concerts, 2,200 private boats greeting and escorting the boats, and elected officials on hand to partake in the festivities. Finally, people from Atlantic City, Avalon, Ocean City, Stone Harbor, and other Jersey cities could reach the other side of the Delaware River and save the trip up the Parkway and down the New Jersey Turnpike to reach points south. Similarly, people who lived in Rehoboth, Dewey, and Bethany Beaches in Delaware, Ocean City (Maryland), and even the Tidewater area of Virginia could avoid the traffic congestion through and around Washington, DC, Baltimore, and Philadelphia to reach points north.

Despite positive projections of the number of passengers and revenues, figures from the first months were less than stellar. A strike by ferry workers didn't help, and the lack of a complete infrastructure at both terminals added to the problems. Once under way, however, the boats ran twenty-four hours a day.

Eventually, traffic did build, says DiPaolo, and it was "amazing what happened in five or six years. It really opened up the peninsula and made it remarkably easy to reach places. Lots of people remember their first crossing."

Between 1972 and 1981, five new diesel-powered ships were constructed and put into service, replacing the older vessels. The MV *Twin Capes,* MV *Delaware,* MV *Cape May,* MV *New Jersey,* and the MV *Cape Henlopen* are all wheelchair accessible, have elevators, air-conditioning, and televisions, and are scheduled to operate 365 days a year. In 1994 the DRBA approved $54.4 million in upgrades to refurbish the fleet. Passengers were now given the opportunity to enjoy indoor and outdoor sitting decks, restaurants, bars, and lounges. The terminals were upgraded in 2000 and 2001 to allow easier access to foot passengers and offer restaurants, lounges, and gift shops.

In what could be a chicken and egg situation, service and ridership have decreased. Starting in 1975, the ferries only operated sixteen hours a day, and now the boats only make four trips each way during the off-season (fifteen trips each way during the summer season).

As ridership has decreased since the peak in 1999, the MV *Cape May* and the MV *Twin Capes* were put on the market, the former in July 2007 and the latter in July 2010. These ships are more labor-intensive than the other three in the fleet, needing more crew members to operate, using more fuel, and having more surface area to maintain.

Still in the fleet today another use has been found for one of these ferries—as a research vessel. A cooperative effort between the University of Delaware's College of Earth, Ocean, and Environment (CEOE) and the DRBA had the MV *Twin Capes* being used to collect water quality data as it plied the mouth of the Delaware Bay, checking temperature, salinity, dissolved oxygen, and chlorophyll content. The information was also sent to the National Oceanic and Atmospheric Administration, which funded the project.

Although not needed during 2012's Hurricane Sandy, in addition to their regular duties, the other ferries have been considered as a means of evacuation when a hurricane is predicted for the area. The low-lying southern Jersey Shore has a limited highway capability, and they would probably flood in a major rain event. There are no storm shelters in the Shore area and residents and tourists are required to evacuate in advance of even a category one hurricane. The threat of a category two or more would cause the ferries to be moved upriver to either Philadelphia or Wilmington, but most likely without passengers. If passengers were taken aboard, it would be without vehicles because there's no place at either port to offload them. As the ferries carry only about one thousand life jackets each, the option is not seen as efficient or effective. It has been suggested that additional life jackets be purchased and warehoused for an eventual storm action.

As the DRBA authority includes the Delaware Memorial Bridge, the Cape May–Lewes Ferry, several small airports, and another ferry, continued Cape May–Lewes Ferry service seems assured even if it's operating at a deficit.

The seventeen-mile trip takes about 80 to 85 minutes, depending on the weather and sea conditions, and it offers drivers and passengers a chance to stretch or take a nap and relieve the tedium of the long drive. Each ferry carries about one hundred cars, trucks, buses, recreational vehicles, tractor trailers, motorcycles, and bikes and has a capacity of one thousand passengers. On Mondays in July and August, a docent from the Lewes Historical Society provides a shipboard history program.

Ted Becker, deputy mayor and treasurer of the Lewes City Council, says the "ferry is viewed as a major benefit here" and notes that the newer ferries have space for rent for events such as the kick-off of the annual United Way campaign in late 2011. His Inn at Canal Square "participates in a program to promote using the ferry to visit both areas." Passengers can see three lighthouses during the crossing, the Cape May Light in New Jersey, and the Harbor of Refuge Light and the Delaware Breakwater East End Light, both near Lewes, and watch dolphins frolicking in season. While the beaches, Cape Henlopen State Park, and Fort Delaware State Park are popular destinations on the Delaware side. About fifteen thousand foot passengers (and an unknown number of people in vehicles) a year use the free shuttle to head for the Tanger Outlet Center where there is no sales tax in the Delaware stores.

That's probably a use that no one considered as ferry crossing plans were conceived over the centuries.

FLY ME TO THE MOON

1965

Whether you're an astronaut, cosmonaut, or some other being who's headed out to space, you need protection in the form of a space suit. You've seen the science fiction films where some innocent (or bad) guy is tossed out of the spaceship screaming as his body rolls over and over, expanding beyond control, and then dies from lack of oxygen or another ghastly cause.

Realistically, the space suit must protect the astronaut from solar radiation and impact from micro meteorites and other debris traveling at thirty thousand miles an hour. It must be able to withstand wide temperature ranges, particularly when the astronaut is outside of the spaceship and depending on whether he is facing the sun or in the shade. It has to be water-cooled to keep an even body temperature or the astronaut will overheat and be easily exhausted.

As we know from the 1967 *Apollo 1* accident when a cabin fire killed three astronauts, it must be nonflammable. Still, it has to provide enough pressurization that the astronaut's blood continues to circulate, and it must supply oxygen for breathing. When flying in one of the National Aeronautic and Space Administration's Apollo missions, the suits had to be small enough, particularly across the shoulders, so the three astronauts could fit inside the capsule. The suits used for previous missions were too big.

Rather than looking like a roly-poly Michelin Man, the suit must be mobile and flexible while pressurized so the astronaut could move about while walking on the moon or trying to fix something on the shuttle or even jumping and leaping from one piece of moonscape to another. Or, like Alan Shepherd, who took a practice golf swing with a six iron on his *Apollo 15* mission.

Those were some of the problems ILC Dover, based in Frederica, faced in 1965 when they started to design and create the space suits for every astronaut who would fly the Apollo missions since *Apollo 7*, including the dozen who walked on the moon. With the backpack for those outdoor excursions, the suit weighed 180 pounds on earth, but only 30 pounds on the moon.

Bill Ayrey, the company's historian, has worked for ILC for since 1978, spending time in the test lab, calibration, and production. Now, he delights in telling the tale of the suit and ILC. He's also the answer person or go-to guy for a movie about the suits being written by Tom McNulty and John Hoberg (producer of the TV series *My Name is Earl*) and produced by Universal. (Ayrey says he's been promised a part as a background extra.) The movie is based on the book *Spacesuit: Fashioning Apollo* by Nicholas de Monchaux.

Teflon had been invented, but the suits were made of fiberglass and the strands of that were coated with Teflon. Velcro was used to make sure things stayed together in the zero gravity of space. Otherwise, any unattached object, like a food pouch, would just float around if it didn't have Velcro on the outside of the package to stick it to a wall.

In the Apollo days, each suit was custom made to fit each astronaut. One astronaut would have longer legs or arms than another. These were not "off the rack" space suits. ILC would go to Houston to take about one hundred measurements of each astronaut, and after about a month the astronauts would fly to Delaware so they could have final fittings where things could be laced tighter to make them snugger, or loosened if more room was needed. Three suits—training, flight, and backup—were made for each astronaut and each backup astronaut. One of the company's proudest moments, says Ayrey, was July 20, 1969, when (the late) Neil Armstrong, wearing an ILC space suit, took man's first step on the moon. You can see one of these suits at the Smithsonian Institution's Apollo exhibit at the National Air and Space Museum in Washington, DC.

Once the moon missions ended in December 1972, ILC space suits were used in Skylab and the Apollo Soyuz Test Project. By 1977, the company was charged with developing the shuttle space suit, which is made with modular units. The upper torso comes in medium, large, and extra large, and then there's a selection of arms and other pieces that are interchangeable and can be switched out depending on the astronaut's size and shape.

ILC helped solve other problems. They had to design and make the suits the astronauts wore when they repaired and replaced the heavy-duty hardware on the Hubble telescope. Suits had to be designed for use on the International Space Station.

With a goal of deeper space exploration, ILC received a contract from NASA's Jet Propulsion Lab (JPL) to develop and build the airbag impact landing system for the Mars Pathfinder Mission. When the Pathfinder landed on Mars on July 4, 1997, it landed softly and safely without using a rocket to lower the vehicle to the surface. Once the lander stopped rolling and bouncing, the airbag-type balloon was programmed to collapse. Six years later, Spirit and Opportunity, the Mars Exploration Rover (MER) missions, settled on Mars with the ILC bags cushioning the landing.

ILC has other closer-to-earth components as it designs and produces the softgoods for blimps, airships, and other lighter-than-air vehicles that you see covering golf tournaments and other events. They have made a 1.3-million-cubic-foot (bigger than the proverbial football field) unmanned airship for the military that will travel at 70,000 feet and be anywhere around the world within ten days, all by remote control. This airship has the capability of seeing a person hiding behind a bush from 186 miles away. Other airships are used for drug interdiction across the Mexican border and over the Caribbean waters. Their use in Afghanistan where they patrol looking for insurgents planting IEDs (improvised explosive devices) along the roadside have saved innumerable lives.

On the ground, Ayrey says a new challenge came in creating a protective garment that could be used by Environmental Protective Agency inspectors who have to examine industrial spills (think about the movie *E.T. The Extra-Terrestrial*). Other suits are used in laboratories where hazardous chemicals are being used. Instead of having the lab employees wear protective gear that caused them to go through safety locks or undress and dress whenever they went for lunch, a bathroom break, or home, the chemicals are encapsulated. This made working conditions easier and safer and eliminated the possibility that a worker might accidentally contaminate the raw materials and pharmaceuticals.

Obviously, the world changed with the development of the space suit and has continued changing with other items essential to many aspects of everyday life today and into the future. And it's happening in tiny Frederica.

STONE BALLOON

1972

As our country was easing into the 1970s, it was reeling from the divisive effects of the Vietnam War and just starting to recover from the shock of the assassinations of John F. Kennedy, Martin Luther King Jr., and Robert F. Kennedy.

The town of Newark, Delaware, was aging as about half of the downtown stores and businesses sat empty. A time-worn Merrill's Tavern and Package Store, at 115 East Main Street, was just about the only busy spot in town, and that wasn't saying much.

I-95 had opened in 1963 with Newark almost halfway between Wilmington and Philadelphia to the northeast and Baltimore and Washington to the southwest. Suddenly, the world could speed by without a glance at or a thought of the town a mile to the north.

The pendulum started swinging the other way on a snowy February 22, 1972, night when people started lining up to enter the new Stone Balloon bar. It was the name that William "Bill" Stevenson gave his bar when he bought Merrill's the previous year. His pursuit of the bar had started when he attended the Woodstock Festival with 500,000 other people in August of 1969, and he decided he wanted to be involved with the world of rock and roll music.

Leading him to Merrill's was a serendipitous inheritance from an uncle he never knew existed. Bill had decided that he loved playing college football but didn't care for college so he dropped out of during his first year. When he bought the bar in the "rickety old building," at the age of twenty-three, he wasn't old enough to own a liquor license, so he had to put it in his mother's name.

To bring the building up to code, he waged a several-months-long frustrating battle with building inspectors and other bureaucrats that called for demolishing half the building. With the drain on his finances and an increasing payroll, he had to borrow money on opening night so the bartenders could make change.

A local band, Iron Hill, was the first of hundreds of bands to perform there. Local bands, including Jack of Diamonds, Dakota (which famed agent Clive Davis heard at the Stone Balloon and signed to a contract), Shytown, and others would become regulars. Other groups played on their way up in popularity or in their waning days, including Bruce Springsteen, Pat Benatar, Larry Tucker, Blue Oyster Cult, Bonnie Raitt, Todd Rundgren, Robert Palmer, Dr. John, the Average White Band, Canned Heat, Chaka Kahn, the Eurythmics, Cheap Trick, Meat Loaf, Paul Revere and the Raiders, Hall and Oates, Chubby Checker, Blood, Sweat and Tears, David Crosby, and Tiny Tim. Both the Buoys and Stanley Steamer, each one-hit wonders, appeared at the bar in the early days.

Stevenson loved to drive (and still does), and he'd spend hours upon hours going to hear one band after another. No group played at the Stone Balloon that hadn't been vetted by Stevenson. He supported local musicians and earned their everlasting loyalty. They'd promote his bar as much as he'd promote their music. Within a short time, every local band in the Newark and Wilmington, Delaware, and nearby Cecil County, Maryland, area knew they had to play at the bar.

After several building additions, the bar could hold about eleven hundred people. That made it larger than the normal live-music joint while not as big as a sports stadium. Newark being so close to the I-95 corridor helped attract bands that might normally ignore the Balloon. It gave them the opportunity to fill in gig nights between other venues as they played up and down the East Coast.

Mitch Hill, a noted area radio personality at the time, says the bar was known by bands from all parts of the world. He'd be backstage with a band in Philly or elsewhere and someone would ask where he was from. When he said Delaware, they'd say, "Oh yeah, Stone Balloon." One of his more distinct memories is of George Thorogood, a local boy whose father worked for DuPont, standing in front of the Balloon, entertaining the patrons while they waited to get into the bar, playing for tips. Hill calls the bar a "darn good example of pre-modern-day taverns and bars. It was a blueprint for clubs around the country by introducing local acts before other bars did. Other people [bar owners] were watching."

Maria Hess, editor of *Delaware Today* magazine, says Stevenson and the Stone Balloon were "basically the greatest rock and roll ambassador and they put Delaware on the rock world map."

By far, the biggest crowds came from the University of Delaware, which was within walking distance of the bar. It was known as a party school with somewhat lax entrance requirements. It didn't have its own music and bar scene, though. According to Stevenson, about 70 percent of the student body came from somewhere else in the country, so they talked about the Newark bar and the performers they'd heard when they went home, helping spread the word. He guesses about two thousand people would pass through the bar in an average week. The bar had souvenir T-shirts, so there have been several hundred thousand of them traveling the world. Stevenson says he was in the Bahamas a few years ago and looked up to see someone wearing a tenth anniversary Stone Balloon T-shirt.

Stevenson created new ways to promote the bar, the talent, and the town. He installed "three pay telephones outside the front door." People would pay their $2 cover charge, come in and enjoy the night's band, and go outside to call their friends to join them, with a "Hey, you won't believe what's happening." This, of course, was in the days before cell phones, Twitter, and Facebook.

He found other ways to make running the bar easier, ideas that were then borrowed by other bars. He built an elevated loading dock so beer distributors could easily roll kegs inside. Budweiser said it was one of the best-selling bars in the country. Bands could unload their equipment with ease. He added more rooms and bars, a sound booth, and an outdoor patio. He provided parking lots so other business owners wouldn't be upset with people parking in their lots or spaces. An accessible ramp was installed, primarily for returning Vietnam veterans using wheelchairs, long before ADA compliance required such things.

Although he hired some college students, he also hired locals, college graduates, returning veterans, and off-duty police. His bar was the first to hire African-American bartenders. He also started providing rides for those who were too intoxicated to drive. He says that cost the bar about $10,000 during his ownership and garnered a great deal of respect and admiration. This was ten years before the formation of Mothers Against Drunk Driving. Borrowing an idea from the famed Studio 54 in New York, he created a newsletter and a hotline. MTV broadcast live from the bar, and *Playboy* magazine named it one of the top college bars in the country. *Rolling Stone* magazine called it the "best-kept secret in rock 'n' roll."

The hundreds of people in line opening night that overfilled the legal capacity was just the first of many such incidents. Stevenson says they were cited for overcrowding about five hundred times. Of course, every time they were fined the news made the front page of the papers and went out over the airwaves, which gave it more publicity.

It seems safe to say the Stone Balloon kept the town of Newark bustling along until the town reached a comfortable age of self-sustained existence and maturity.

For several reasons, Stevenson said goodbye to his bar in 1985. For two decades afterward it muddled through, but the writing was on the wall. The university had toughened the entrance standards and upgraded its scholastic reputation so students weren't partying quite as much as they used to. Music fans could buy (or download for free) single cuts off the Internet and not have to buy full albums. The final balloon dropped on December 17, 2005, when the building was sold and then razed the following June. Upscale condominiums and a few commercial enterprises were erected in its place, including a new Stone Balloon Winehouse with food and beverages and a Tuscan-themed decor. The condo market is primarily older and retired residents, not beer-guzzling youngsters.

Decades after Stevenson first opened the door, people still recall the Stone Balloon and the fun they had there. Reunions have been held, attracting three hundred or more people. Stevenson says the Stone Balloon was the bridge that connected college students, townies, and musicians from around the world.

PUNKIN CHUNKIN

1986

In 1986, John Ellswort, the late Trey Melson, Bill Thompson, and Donald "Doc" Pepper were sitting around on the first Saturday after Halloween when pumpkins were plentiful and cheap, and time was weighing idly on their hands. They thought it would be fun to see how far they could toss a pumpkin. They had enough fun that they promised to meet the following year and then again the following year.

No one could have known that this bit of mischief would be the framework of the World Championship Punkin Chunkin Association (WCPCA). Now, thousands upon thousands of people come annually to the town of Bridgeville, Delaware, a community of 2,048 (according to the 2010 census). They amass on a one-thousand-acre farm that sees more than one hundred teams vie for the honor of the farthest chunk. On the weekend of the first Saturday of November, spectators come from around the country and even from a foreign country or two. They huddle together against the cold and sometimes rainy weather for three days of pumpkin flinging, good food, entertainment, and a chance to renew friendships from one year to the next.

Frank Shade, a paramedic, volunteer firefighter, founder of the Sussex County Cancer Survivors Fund, board member of the Lower Delaware Autism Foundation, and county employee, is former president and now the spokesman for the Chunkin Association. He says if you do a search for pumpkin tossing events, you'll probably find an almost endless list of them scheduled in every little town, by every Boy Scout troop, all trying to raise funds by seeing how far they can throw a gourd.

Some of them are licensed by the WCPCA. "We don't want to see anyone get hurt," says Shade, so they offer services and suggestions about how the event should be run.

Over the years the Chunk grew. More teams entered. Divisions were established that include catapults, slingshots, trebuchet, torsion, human powered, and pneumatic air cannon. Some of the cannons measure 120 feet, longer than the longest first toss, which was 114 feet. The land is surveyed and designated with GPS markings to facilitate measuring how long each shot is. Riders on ATVs go out to the landing spot and mark it with a colored spray paint, with each team having a color to differentiate them. Each team has one shot on each of the three days of the competition.

As the event grew, people started lighting a few barbecue grills, cooking, and giving away food. Then food vendors became involved. Gradually, other activities were added, including fireworks, a pumpkin-cooking contest, a chili-cooking contest, amusement rides, a Miss Punkin Chunkin contest, and live concerts. The pumpkin and chili recipes do not have to be original and are collected in a Punkin Chunkin recipe book that's available for sale.

The Chunk has become a huge production, taking 2,500 to 3,500 people to help erect safety fences, put up portable toilets, keep everything running smoothly and on time, taking down everything after the Chunk is finished. All of them volunteer their services.

Cable television networks, including Discovery and the Science Channel, cover the event and in 2011 Kari Byron, Grant Imahara, and Tory Belleci from *Mythbusters* handled the interviews and chunk-by-chunk coverage, producing about four hours of television broadcast time. Shade says the people from Sharp Entertainment, the company that produces the television coverage, tell him it's the largest event they've ever covered.

Shade says, "The participants do it for the love of the event and bragging rights. There are no monetary awards." And they spend a lot of money creating their machines, traveling, staying in hotels in nearby Seaford and beyond, and eating at local restaurants. Spectators return annually to follow their favorite teams, even seeking autographs and photographs with their beloved chunkers.

The WCPCA provides about four thousand to five thousand pumpkins (one and a half to two tractor loads) every year for the event, but most teams bring their own, as many as a dozen or more pumpkins. They have to be round or at least roundish, weigh between eight and ten pounds, and be able to survive the chunk. Generally, Caspers, Luminas, and La Estrellas are the favored varieties because of their thick skin or rind that holds up well under the pressure of the chunk. A pumpkin that falls apart before it hits the ground is called a Pie, as in (pumpkin) pie in the sky.

Almost inevitably someone says the pumpkins should be donated to hungry people. Shade says they always tell people that they'll provide two pumpkins for every one they throw if the people who want them will pay for the shipping. No takers, yet.

With so many people from so many walks of life involved, it's not surprising that couples have met and that three or four weddings have been performed at the Chunk and one couple admitted to conceiving a child there; the three-month-old attended the following Chunk.

The distance goal is a mile, but that hasn't been met at this Chunk. Such variables as wind, temperature, humidity, and the condition of the crop (2011 pumpkins were somewhat soft due to the weather and growing conditions) affect how high and far the pumpkin will travel. A pneumatic air cannon named "Big 10 Inch" did shoot a pumpkin 5,545.43 feet on September 9, 2010, in Moab, Utah. It is listed in the *Guinness Book of World Records* as of January 2011. However, Moab is at a higher elevation, the air thinner, and the chunk is downhill.

According to Scott Thomas, executive director of the Southern Delaware Tourism office, of those who attend, nearly half spend the night at a hotel, condo, campground, or with friends and family. A survey taken at the 2010 event showed that most of them stay for two nights, although some stay for four or five, and they find accommodations in Lewes, Georgetown, Rehoboth, Seaford, Millsboro, and other towns. Most are locals, but people come from as far away as Connecticut to the north, Florida to the south, and Arizona and Washington to the west. Whether visiting in person or catching one of the television shows, this provides an immediate tourism impact for the usually slow November. It also gives a distant bang for the buck in the following months and years.

Perhaps more important than the fun, camaraderie, bragging rights, and tourism boost, the organization has raised hundreds of thousands of dollars for nonprofit organizations. These funds come from team registration, vendor fees, admission fees, and other sources. Among the charities that have received donations are the Autism Foundation, Bless Our Children, Bridgeville Volunteer Fire Department, Child Help, Home of the Brave, Lewes (and Rehoboth) Meals on Wheels, St. Baldrick's Foundation, and St. Jude

Children's Research Hospital. Others may be added for a year or two, particularly when they are having a short-term financial problem.

Additionally, local churches, boys and girls clubs, and almost any organization, even if it isn't officially recognized as a charitable group, can receive funds. This is particularly true if they participate in the function. Also, nonperishable food items are collected and donated to the needy.

A scholarship fund was established during those early years requiring that the recipients had to be local students and had to announce a major in agri-science, engineering, or some other pumpkin-related educational field. Those rules were modified and scholarships are given to almost every student who applies, based primarily upon need, but with some preference going to Delaware residents and those who help run the Chunk or work on one of the chunk teams. In 2011 they awarded $40,000 in scholarships to nearly two dozen students.

Shade says their goal is to send a check to an organization, such as St. Jude's, until it's returned, "Because the problem is fixed."

"Where else," asks Shade, "can you have this much fun and raise this much money?"

LIGHT THE LIGHTS

1995

A major disadvantage to historic old things is they are old. They are fragile, deteriorate, fade, crumble, and generally fall apart. All you need is the wrong combination of air, humidity, and light (particularly ultraviolet and infrared), and *voila!*, the painting, letter, photograph, material, and other treasures are gone. At best, you might have digital images, but they aren't the same when trying to convey the past. Even if fragility isn't an issue, the heat generated by lighting has to be cooled, which requires excessive energy consumption. The only solution was to rotate exhibits or hide the valuables in a dark room where they couldn't be exposed to the elements or seen.

That's where Ruth Ellen Miller and her dad, Jack V. Miller, entered the picture. For the museum and similar worlds, they created the better mouse trap or the best thing since sliced bread. Ruth Ellen, a magna cum laude business graduate from California Polytechnic University in Pomona, California, with a bent for art and design, started worrying about photochemical damage to valuable artifacts. Her dad, a scientist and optical engineer with more than a hundred patents to his name, shared her concern. When you see compact fluorescent lights that don't blink, you know who to thank. He worked on a programmable rocket system that made moon exploration possible, and his genius carried over to the laser mounts for military rifles and battle tanks.

Ruth Ellen also has numerous inventions and patents to her credit, all related to their new lighting system.

The two of them created an illumination system they call NoUVIR (pronounced new veer) that goes into quantum physics, which explores more than the average person needs to know, but results in a fiber-optic light system that is "stone-cold, pure-white fiber optic that has no ultraviolet and no infrared components." It's also smaller than traditional lighting and eliminates the heat generated from typical lighting. The user has "absolute control over aim, focus, and intensity." They work with "Reflected Energy Matching Theory," which they say "has been called the most important advance in conservation science of the century."

Because the lighting systems are small, don't generate any heat, and can be aimed, they can be used in places that are tiny and hard to access. The lights can be hidden so they eliminate glare and distraction.

The Millers have, literally, written the books on the subject, including *Reflected Energy Matching as a Conservation Tool.*

After exploring manufacturing options, they decided Delaware was the best place to start their lighting business and within those boundaries, Seaford was ideal. A prime concern was the production cost because museums and other organizations that would benefit from this type of lighting generally have limited resources. Lower expenses meant the lighting was available to operations that might not be able to afford a more expensive system.

When you stop by the Seaford Historical Society Museum (in the former 1936 post office) on High Street, you're looking at exhibits illuminated by NoUVIR.

Going a little farther afield, the Bata Shoe Museum in Toronto, Ontario, Canada, uses the NoUVIR lighting system with the fiber optics installed in the ceiling. The semi-permanent exhibit includes ninety pairs of shoes, boots, and moccasins created by Native Americans from various areas across the continent. The shoes, made from a variety of different animal skins, some dyed and some not, show the variations in patterns and colors and uses of beadwork, feathers, or pieces of horsehair.

"It's part of their green program," says Ruth Ellen, but equally important: "We're saving the artifacts. Leather will pick up 0.5 percent sulfuric acid in a year from city pollution from cars and from the humidity cycles created by the heat in normal lights. With NoUVIR, the acid erosion is stopped, which is particularly important in leather conservation." As is typical of most of their installations, Ruth Ellen says they save about 70 percent of their former energy costs, and the hardware pays for itself in a little more than two years. She says the Bata comment is appropriate: "We're not green, we're bright green."

Another setting is the historic Hampton Mansion in Towson, Maryland, the first structure purchased by the National Park Service. NoUVIR is used in the dining room, main parlor, and the music room. Similarly, Agecroft Hall, in Richmond, Virginia, a Tudor home from the time of Henry VIII that was picked up and moved from Lancashire, England, to the Old Dominion, has displays lit with NoUVIR.

The Kansas City Speedway Hollywood Casino had incorporated Hollywood-themed exhibits in their decor and is using the lighting system to illuminate a pair of ruby red slippers and Judy Garland's test dress for *The Wizard of Oz,* Daniel Craig's tuxedo from *Casino Royale,* and other items that belonged to Hollywood legend Jean Harlow. The cases are hermetically sealed to prevent deterioration of the items displayed.

Eggs from birds that went extinct centuries ago from the natural history collection at the University of Florida can be displayed now. With the previous lighting system, the shells kept getting thinner and thinner, and while some display items can be replaced or repaired, extinct-bird eggs aren't in that category.

While we're used to seeing Air Force One take to the air, we are hard-pressed to remember that Franklin D. Roosevelt was the first president to fly while in office. His plane, a Douglas VC-54C called the *Sacred Cow,* took him to the Yalta Conference in February 1945 and later flew President Harry S Truman. The plane is wood-lined and has an inlaid seal of the president, all under the NoUVIR lighting. The plane is on display at the National Museum of the US Air Force, Dayton, Ohio.

Other displays you might have seen include Thomas Jefferson's handwritten draft of the Declaration of Independence, Abraham Lincoln's Gettysburg Address, the Bill of Rights, the Louisiana Purchase, and the Magna Carta. You can also see the lighting at the Smithsonian Institution's National Postal Museum, National Prisoner of War Museum, Dallas Museum of Art, Jamestown Visitor Center, the Tusayan Museum (Grand Canyon Visitor Center), and numerous other attractions.

Another problem with traditional lighting is the color isn't true to natural lighting. The Houston Museum of Natural Science has one of the world's largest and finest rock and gem collections. The exhibits include works by Tiffany and an extraordinary jewelry collection. If visitors could see the difference between normal lighting and the NoUVIR system, they'd realize it's like night and day.

Budgets for lighting and electricity are almost as much a concern as conservation, so the Millers are particularly pleased with the bottom line results from their installations. Ruth Ellen says they installed forty systems that replaced seven hundred framing projectors. As each NoUVIR system had thirty-two spotlights that can be individually focused, that gave the museum 1,280 spotlights. Besides looking better, the maintenance costs dropped. Ruth Ellen says that every watt put into a building needs three or four watts of HVAC to remove; the reduced heat let them take an entire chiller off line. That reduced the utility bill by about $8,000 a month for a total saving of $96,000 a year or more than $1,000,000 after eleven years.

Specialized lighting needs go beyond works of art. A shark tank and other aquaria in the Middle East hold mollusks, jellyfish, and other sea life where man and beast are happier and healthier because the lighting lasts about ten times longer than other types of illumination.

And, should you visit the Millers in the twenty-eight room 1836 Victorian Highview House they've had restored, you'll see the results of the fiber-optic lighting they installed throughout the two main floors.

FOR THOSE WHO SERVED

2003

A discreet notice is posted on the Internet whenever the Air Force Mortuary Affairs Operations unit has received approval by the surviving designated family member that the media may cover the return of a fallen military body at Dover Air Force Base.

Media had been prevented from witnessing the transfer of flag-draped boxes since 1991 during the Persian Gulf War, and the policy was reissued in 2001 with the start of Operation Enduring Freedom. This guideline was modified in 2009 by then-Secretary of Defense Robert Gates, who changed the regulation to allow family members the chance to approve media attendance.

The dignified transfer of the remains is one component involved in the detailed process of treating the body with extreme dignity, honor, and respect and to show the families care, service, and support. Another component is the aim to process a body within twenty-four hours so it can be transferred to the family in an expeditious manner.

Wartime deaths—even peacetime ones—are inevitable. The nearly seven dozen military and civilian personnel—up from a mere dozen a decade ago—at the Charles C. Carson Center for Mortuary Affairs, located at the Dover Air Force Base, are charged with the return of all Department of Defense personnel and dependents from overseas contingency operations, other overseas deaths, and mass fatalities that occur within the United States and sometimes elsewhere.

The medical examiners or coroners also receive help from pathologists, anthropologists, forensic photographers, radiologists, and licensed dental technicians from the Office of the Armed Forces Medical Examiners, the Federal Bureau of Investigation, Army Criminal Investigation Division, Air Force Office of Special Investigation, and/or Naval Criminal Investigative Service (NCIS).

Charles C. Carson (1925–2002), who was the mortuary director for twenty-six years, started as a civilian mortician for the US Air Force in 1958, was assigned to Dover in 1970, and retired in 1996. The Carson Center and the street in front of it were named in his honor when the new center was dedicated to replace the facility that had processed more than fifty thousand service members since it opened in 1955. The Carson Center is a $30 million, 73,000-square-foot facility that opened in November 2003 and is our country's only port mortuary and the largest one in the Department of Defense. It's the same facility that's mentioned in Patricia Cornwell's eighteenth book, *Port Mortuary*.

Originally known as the Dover Port Mortuary, the department continues the service of preparing bodies that was started when Dr. Jonathan Letterman created the first triage procedure during the Battle of Antietam in 1862. Over the years, the Dover mortuary has been charged with dealing with or identifying the remains from several major catastrophes. They identified the bodies of 327 Americans who were killed in the air crash at Los Rodeos Airport in Tenerife, Canary Islands, Spain; processed the more than nine hundred victims of the Jonestown, Guyana, suicide/mass murder in 1978; and identified the victims of the space shuttle *Challenger* accident in 1986 and the space shuttle *Columbia* accident in 2003.

They identified the crew members of the *H.L. Hunley* submarine that sank during the Civil War. After the attack on the Pentagon on September 11, 2001, they identified 184 of the 189 people who were killed, including Pentagon employees (civilians and military), children, passengers on Flight 77, and the hijackers. That last task raised the number of employees more than tenfold in just a few days. Now, nearly seven hundred bodies pass through the mortuary every year.

Unfortunately, this is the same mortuary that had several scandals exposed in 2011. In one case, personnel had lost body parts, and in another, remnants had been disposed of in a Virginia landfill. Whistleblowers who brought these mismanagement practices to light were fired or suspended, contrary to current regulations. Three Air Force personnel were reprimanded, demoted, and reassigned.

Fortunately, a few rotten apples are not spoiling the excellent work the mortuary is doing.

The changes in mortuary science have been drastic. In the wise words of Cornwell's fictional character Dr. Kay Scarpetta on the pages of *Port Mortuary,* "They have 3-D imaging radiology, the use of computerized tomography, or CT, scans in the morgue. . . . The traditional postmortem examination dissects as you go and takes photographs after the fact and hopes you don't miss something or introduce an artifact can be dramatically improved by technology and made more precise, and it should be."

The art and science of virtual autopsies were developed by European radiologists who taught the procedure to the US Armed Forces. Among the advantages are lower costs than a full autopsy performed by a doctor, the privacy afforded the body where religious and cultural practices would prohibit a traditional autopsy, and the ability to keep the images on file in perpetuity, files that can be reexamined any time they're needed.

Today's autopsy starts with a scan—similar to airport luggage scanners—to detect any unexploded ordnance, bullets, hand grenades, or other potentially dangerous materials that might blow up, possibly destroying the rest of the body, the autopsy team, and nearby equipment or more. Then the bodies and any body pieces are barcoded. Fingerprints, dental records, photographs, forensic pathology, tissue samples, and digital X-rays are collected for identification purposes. Personal effects are recorded and saved to be returned with the body. Records are checked to determine which awards they're entitled to and where their families live.

The 16-slice CT scan (meaning the machine takes sixteen images with each revolution around the body) takes about fifteen minutes. While it was initially thought it might slow down the process, it has proven to be a necessary part of the process. When body parts are missing, a GE software package called "Stickman" helps fill in the missing pieces, providing a trajectory line of a bullet or other valuable information. The films collected from the scan maintain the body's integrity after it has been opened in a real autopsy.

Among the information they're trying to collect is whether, in the case of head injuries, the correct size helmet was issued to military personnel. This data is important to companies that provide protective gear to the military, which could also include jeeps, tanks, or other military transports. Because they can identify what type of metal is in the body, they can help determine what type of ammunition or bomb caused the death.

Although the CT scan is not absolutely perfect, it has gone a long way in understanding what happened and why. While a virtual autopsy can sometimes miss a bullet track when there are intersecting tracks (from automatic weaponry rather than a single shot from a handgun), the machine can catch fractures and other things not caught in a visual autopsy. It's much better at scanning bones than it is soft tissue.

The CT scan is seen to be as important to saving lives of military personnel as MASH (mobile army surgical hospital) units have been by improving triage and treatments and by determining, from previous fatalities, if someone with a specific injury could survive with different treatment.

Beyond the technical advances that you might see on any police procedural TV show or movie (although time condensed, which lets things happen almost instantaneously), it's the human and humane way the bodies and everything involved in the procedure are handled that deserve your respect and admiration. These are the small details that tell the story of how the events that take place in this center have changed over the years.

In preparation for sending the remains home, uniforms are ironed with properly sharp creases and all brass buttons are highly polished so not even a fingerprint shows. The chrome on a belt buckle shines brighter than any adornment on an automobile. A new ribbon rack is created and each award is placed in its proper position. A bronze star will light up like stars from the sky. And the lettering on the name tag receives a fresh coat of Air Force blue paint, applied with a toothpick. The service personnel who will be put to rest could stand any inspection ever met while on duty.

Overseeing all this, in a special way, are the Port Mortuary chaplains. They are there to help the personnel who perform these tasks and they are there to help counsel the family. When appropriate, they pray over the remains. They talk with the family, laughing at the remembrance of the good times and sharing tears at the loss and thoughts of what might have been.

With the 2009 change of policy that allows media to attend (with family permission), more family members have been attending the transfer ceremony in Dover. That means additional help from the chaplains. It's a job that requires that the chaplains be available day and night. Each chaplain works at the center for four months to make sure he or she can handle the job. After that time, the chaplain can be considered for a long-term assignment, sometimes for a year and sometimes for much longer.

Should you visit the center, the first thing you see when you enter is the Wall of Fallen Heroes where each military event—with the date and the number of fallen heroes—is engraved in the glass so all will remember.

It is the unspoken, and perhaps spoken, hope of all these personnel that the families will soon forget the tears and remember the smiles and the service their loved ones gave to their country.

AUGUSTA FLOATS

2010

Milford is a town that could easily have a split personality. It straddles the scenic banks of the Mispillion River and is sometimes called the Garden City of Twin Counties, Kent and Sussex. It's as pretty a picture-postcard town as you could wish to see and visit. That steadfast calm and tranquility belies its hectic past and its importance to our country's survival. The town was settled somewhere around 1680 and incorporated in 1807; shipbuilding was flourishing there by the last part of the eighteenth century due to water access and an abundant supply of white oak trees.

This story, however, starts almost a century later, in 1896 when shipbuilding was a major industry in this town, which was home to a half-dozen shipyards during the trade's prime. The Vinyard Shipbuilding Company was founded by Wilson M. Vinyard, a Milford native. He built his first gasoline-powered steamboat in 1895–96 in Wisconsin and captained it to Delaware, where he eventually set up the shipyard. His first boat in Milford, the *Mary*

M. Vinyard, was launched in 1904, and that was followed by other wooden cruisers, almost one a year through 1909.

As World War I was approaching, the shipyard converted to building boats for the US Coast Guard. In the decade following 1917, Vinyard built four tugboats and ten seventy-five-foot patrol boats that were used extensively to detect, chase, and detain rumrunners during the height of Prohibition.

By 1927, the shipyard had changed from military construction back to personal yacht building, constructing boats that ranged from ninety to one hundred ten feet long. The yard employed more than five dozen craftsmen, eager to showcase their fine talents.

According to the boatyard's current owner, Joan Lofland (with husband Sudler), Vinyard had met John Trumpy and had been exposed to his master craftsmanship. Trumpy was known for his exquisite boats that had great attention to details and comfort. It's said his boats were owned by the most prestigious and wealthy families in the country. Perhaps his most famous boat was the *Sequoia,* the wooden yacht used by every president from Herbert Hoover to Jimmy Carter. This yacht was built at a cost of $200,000 and was launched in 1926. She was 104 feet long and a shade more than eighteen feet abeam, with a relatively shallow draft of four feet five inches and a speed of twelve knots. Below deck, she had a presidential stateroom, a galley and dining room, and, when used by President Franklin D. Roosevelt, an elevator to assist him in reaching the various decks. She eventually made the US National Register of Historic Places and the US National Historic Landmark list, both on December 23, 1987.

She served as Vinyard's inspiration when he designed and built the *Augusta.* She had some wonderful creature comforts including expensive mahogany interiors, electric lights, refrigeration, propane stove, a full-size sink, and bathrooms (heads). She slept six people comfortably (eight if they knew each other well), plus a forward cabin for the captain. She was fifty feet long and thirteen feet abeam with twin 65 horsepower Kermath engines that propelled the boat up to seventeen miles per hour. The keel was a single piece of white oak and the outside planking was grained Douglas fir. She was launched in July 1927. Vinyard boasted that the yacht was the "greatest cruiser ever built" and "safety and satisfaction were built into the boat."

Starting in 1942, the yard again returned to military boat construction and the workforce rose to 120 men. They built fourteen swift and easily maneuverable 110-foot wooden sub chasers for the US Navy, part of a fleet of 580 boats of the "Splinter Fleet" that were commissioned at various shipyards during the war. The wooden boat was superior, at the time, to a metal-hulled one because trees and supplies were readily available almost everywhere and wooden boats could be built much more quickly, and almost anywhere, than metal boats that needed full metal shops for construction. That left shipyards that could make metal ships available to produce other types of vessels.

The sub chasers were armed with depth charges, machine guns, and antiaircraft guns. They helped escort and protect boats in the Atlantic and Pacific against German and Japanese submarines, sinking more than five dozen German U-boats during the war. They were also used in amphibious landings in Europe and the Pacific. The Vinyard boats were faster and broader than previous boats built for similar uses. They had better engines and were made of the hardest wood so they could withstand the punishment of rough seas and tough battles. Of those boats, two went to the USSR in 1945, two to the Dominican Republic in 1947, and one to the Philippines in 1948.

The yard was closed after the war and then operated for two decades, starting in the 1960s, as Delaware Marine & Manufacturing.

As fiberglass and mass production replaced the hand-crafted vessels of old, the boatyard ceased operation once again.

Fortunately, the Loflands found and bought the home and boatyard in 1996 and have been working on restoring the old buildings and other Vinyard boats, the *Kismet* (1938) and the *Vignette* (1951), saving them from Davey Jones' locker or worse.

They acquired the fifty-foot *Augusta* in 2009, rescuing it from a dry dock in Tappahanock, Virginia. They spent nine months transforming the broken engines, rotten hull, and other furnishings, making her seaworthy. That involved numerous little and big projects, including the conversion of the boat from twin engines to one—while keeping the horsepower rating and speed the same—and adding such creature comforts as a microwave oven, air-conditioning, a new steering system, and other items that would have been difficult to fit and install in the boat if they hadn't rescued space by replacing one engine.

The newly restored *Augusta* was launched among appropriate pomp and circumstance on Saturday, June 12, 2010, with Joan and Sudler Lofland, historian and author Dave Kenton, other representatives from the Milford Museum, and lots of people who had spent countless hours working on this fine lady in attendance. Now, today's generation of seafarers and future sailors can see and appreciate the beauty of a boat that's more than ninety years old. The Loflands plan to convert four rooms of the old Vinyard paymaster's office into a small tourist center to help explain how the ships were built and what factors were incorporated into their designs. Who knows who the next master craftsman (or woman) will be and what contributions he or she will make to the wonderful world of sailing and Milford's nautical history?

AND IT HUFFS AND IT PUFFS

2010

A gas shortage in 1973 caused by an Arab oil embargo, current and constant increasing gas prices because of increased demand in China and other expanding countries, and global warming warnings, among other issues, have sent out enough alarms that some people are looking for other means of generating power from fossil fuels. The alarm from consumers wasn't too loud even a dozen years ago, for oil was still only $25 a barrel as late as the year 2000. However, in Delaware in late 2005, a seven-year price cap was removed from electricity prices. Suddenly, the price of electricity rose, as was expected. What also should have been expected was the increase in price of everything that was made with electricity in any way, from bread to tires and beyond.

In addition to the financial costs, the largest air pollutants are power generation and transportation. Find another inexpensive or relatively inexpensive way to generate power and perhaps the world will beat a path to your door.

That's when the citizens of Delaware and its general assembly enacted a measure calling for the state to generate more of its own power, particularly wind power. An exhaustive study was conducted that included comments from almost 3,500 citizens, with nearly ten to one in favor of wind power, even if it meant paying more in electricity bills. Yet wind turbine power is less expensive than solar energy. Even the coastal beach towns, where views toward the ocean might be affected, endorsed the concept.

Estimates came in that an offshore wind turbine farm would provide hundreds of new union jobs—about $100,000,000 in direct wages and spin-off industries—and eliminate several outdated coal-fired power plants, saving the state about $750,000,000 in health-care expenses. It would also establish a constant charge for power for twenty-five years rather than constantly increasing costs of coal-fired plants.

Because the coastal areas from northern Virginia to Maine have high population concentrations and little room for building land-based turbine farms, other areas along the East Coast, including Maine, New Jersey, New York, and Rhode Island, were considering the use of offshore wind power. Additionally, off-shore winds are more constant and stronger.

The University of Delaware, College of Earth, Ocean, and Environment, Hugh R. Sharp Campus in Lewes, has been at the forefront of the research. In 2008, the university and the Ontario, New York–based Sustainable Energy Developments, Inc. studied the viability of installing a commercial-grade turbine on the campus. You can see the result when you visit the campus and see the 256-foot-tall wind turbine. Construction of the two-megawatt Gamesa wind turbine began on March 20, 2010, and was completed in June 2010. The process took fifty loads of cement, sixty tons of rebar, and a large crane to set it in place.

Weighing in at 203 tons, the three blades are each 144 feet long (each weighing seven tons), and the nacelle (the part in the middle where the blades meet that holds the mechanical and electrical parts) alone accounts for 103 tons. It's made of epoxy reinforced with carbon and glass fibers. When it's rotating, it can go from nine to nineteen revolutions per minute and it rotates clockwise so the wind blows it into position. It cuts out when winds reach forty-five miles per hour or above. In its first year, the turbine produced 5.1 million kilowatt hours (kWh) of energy, enough to power the Lewes campus and have 1.3 million kWh left over that was directed to the Lewes Board of Public Works to power about 120 homes and buildings. This is the first utility-scale turbine in the state.

The campus was chosen because of its proximity to the Atlantic Ocean and Delaware Bay. As the sun heats the earth at a different rate than it does the nearby bodies of water, there is a variation of air temperatures that creates air movement or wind. This creates kinetic energy, which is captured by the turbine's vanes or blades and is then converted to mechanical energy, which turns a generator that makes electric energy. Whether you think of the Netherlands and their windmills or Don Quixote, it's a principle that's been implemented for centuries.

Installing the turbine had a twofold purpose. One, it provides all the power the university needs in a carbon-free mode (with extra power going into the grid for the nearby town of Lewes). Second, it offers an excellent teaching and research mechanism regarding whether or how the turbine affects birds and bats, how the corrosive power of the salty air affects the machinery, how the turbine survives Nor'easters and hurricanes, and other factors. This information is invaluable to undergraduate and graduate science and engineering students who are studying wind energy toward receiving a Wind Energy Certificate. The school also offers courses in solar energy, fuel cells, energy policy, climate change, sustainable energy, and other research projects through the University of Delaware Energy Institute. These students will help lead us into a more sustainable energy-driven world.

And the research will help with a proposed offshore wind turbine, the first in the Americas.

A 2007 survey report indicated the wind resources available off the Atlantic Ocean shoreline could provide the energy needed from Massachusetts to North Carolina and have plenty left over for future needs.

Although there is fairly common agreement that wind power would be beneficial in our efforts to eliminate fossil fuels and reliance upon imported oil, finding the perfect onshore or offshore location has been a problem. In late 2010, the University of Delaware started looking for a site to test offshore wind power turbines, located as close as within three miles of land that's under state control and farther out, up to about thirteen miles offshore, in waters that are federally controlled. They had eliminated the Delaware Bay area because it is an important migratory route for shorebirds and waterfowl.

Offshore wind is projected to be more expensive than onshore wind, if only because the ocean bottom is deeper so construction costs will be higher. Yet the contemplated array of 49 to 150 wind turbines off the Delaware coast is projected to provide enough electricity to power more than fifty thousand energy users for a renewable energy standard of 25 percent by 2025.

Whether federal funding and subsidies will be available is the question that seems to be holding up any project development. As construction costs of offshore wind power is about 2.45 times the cost of building an onshore wind turbines and six times the cost of constructing a natural-gas plant, they can't compete yet against other resources.

Although many wind turbine farms and individual turbines have been installed and are being used around the country and on other parts of the planet, Delaware became the first state to request proposals (RFP) for offshore wind energy generation. Bill 6 of the 143rd General Assembly, 2006–2007, calls for a new power plant that received three bids, the selection of a winning bidder, and an agreement for power purchase. Two sites were selected, Atlantic North and Atlantic South, which would produce 600 MW, of which Delmarva Power would buy 200 MW with the rest available to sell to other jurisdictions. With federal budget cuts affecting such projects, Bluewater, which had won the contract, and its parent company, NRG Energy, have decided not to invest yet, so there is no Delaware project in the works. Another small kink has been the increased efficiency of appliances, electronics, and other items in our everyday life and work that has reduced some of the demand on electricity.

Dr. Willett Kempton, marine policy professor, notes that Delaware's affirmative action to use wind turbines, requiring Delmarva Power to buy the wind-generated power, "was the first of any state and influenced many neighboring states to take action." Eventually, this Power Purchase Agreement (PPA) for offshore wind may prove to be the sea change that is necessary to jump-start the mass use of off-shore wind turbine farms.

STATE FACTS AND TRIVIA

- Statehood: December 7, 1787, the First State

- Capital: Dover

- Total Area: 49th among states (Rhode Island is smallest), 2,490 square miles

- Width: 30 miles

- Length: 96 miles

- Largest City: Wilmington

- Number of Counties: Three (New Castle, Kent, Sussex, from north to south)

- Highest Point: Near Ebright Azimuth, 447.85 feet (136.5 meters); second only to Florida for having the lowest high elevation

- Total Population: 45th among states (2011 estimate 907,135; sixth in density with 442.6 people per square mile)

- State Bird: Blue Hen chicken

- State Butterfly: Tiger swallowtail

- State Colors: Colonial blue and buff

- State Dessert: Peach pie

- State Drink: Milk

- State Fish: Weakfish (also known as sea trout, gray trout, yellow mouth, and yellowfin trout)

- State Flower: Peach blossom

- State Fossil Shell: Belemnite

- State Fruit: Strawberry

- State Herb: Sweet goldenrod

- State Insect: Ladybug

- State Marine Animal: Horseshoe crab

- State Mineral: Sillimanite

- State Motto: Liberty and Independence

- State Nicknames: First State, Blue Hen State (or Blue Hen Chicken State), Chemical Capital, Corporate Capital), Small Wonder, Diamond

- State Slogan: It's Good Being First

- State Song: "Our Delaware" (words by George Hynson and music by William Brown)

- State Star: Delaware Diamond

- State Tree: American holly

- State Wildlife Animal: Gray fox

- Delaware was the first of the thirteen colonies to ratify the Constitution of the United States, on December 7, 1787, thus taking on the title of the First State. Because of this, Delaware is first at many national events, including presidential inauguration parades.

- Captain Henry Hudson, sailing the *Half Moon,* is credited with being the first European to find the entrance to Delaware Bay on August 28, 1609. He was an Englishman who was hired by the Dutch.

- Samuel Argall, another English sea captain, named the bay and river for Thomas West, Third Baron De La Warr, an English nobleman and the first colonial governor of Virginia.

- Wilmington was founded in 1731 and named Willington by Thomas Willing. It was renamed in 1739.

- Dutch colonists established Zwaanendael (now Lewes) in 1631. The community was destroyed and all thirty-two inhabitants were killed by the Lenni-Lenape Indians in 1632. Lewes is the self-proclaimed "First Town in the First State" because it was the first European settlement in the state. It is named after the town of Lewes, England, and both towns are in their respective county of Sussex.

- Gore-Tex, the breathable waterproof fabric that's used in such things as dental floss, guitar strings, and fabrics, was co-invented in 1969 by Wilbert L. Gore, Rowena Taylor, and Robert W. Gore, Wilbert's son, in Newark. The W. L. Gore Company now employs about nine thousand people (called associates) in thirty countries.

- The first peach orchard was planted in 1832. By 1932, the apple crop (primarily in Kent and Sussex Counties) produced between 9 and 14 percent of the state's total fruit value.

- Mrs. Mollie Brown-Rust and her nineteen second grade students of the Lulu M. Ross Elementary School in Milford started the drive to have the ladybug named the official state bug. Ladybugs are noted for their ability to eat tiny insects that damage plants, consuming up to sixty aphids a day. They aren't exactly particular about their diets and will also eat mealy bugs, leaf hoppers, mites, and other soft insects. The ladybug was adopted by the legislature on April 25, 1974. Twenty-five years later, the school's second grade class realized the state Internet page didn't credit the students or the school for their effort, so this class petitioned the webmaster to include that information and it was added in 2000. Milford holds an annual Bug and Bud Festival with parades, ladybug crafts, and other entertainments.

- Delaware is small enough that in 1963, Alan Funt and his *Candid Camera* TV program set up a roadblock that fooled a lot of people. On a two-lane road from Pennsylvania into the First State, a sign told all drivers of cars with out-of-state license plates that Delaware was closed for the day. People turned around and went back toward the Keystone State.

- Roughly, rain falling south of Route 2 and Business 2 (between Newark and Wilmington) drains into the Delaware River and Bay before feeding into the Atlantic Ocean, and rain falling north of that line drains into the Chesapeake Bay before joining the Atlantic.

- The bald cypress trees that grow at Trap Pond State Park are thought to be the northernmost growth of these trees.

- Milton used to be a center of ice harvesting, producing enough to provide for the area and ship south where they didn't have frozen ponds or lakes. No, the Delaware Bay is salt water and that rarely freezes over, and certainly not deep enough to have been part of the harvest. Once electric refrigerators were built, the industry died except in the occasional museum exhibit or historical demonstration.

- John Dickinson (1732–1808) was a lawyer, a militia officer during the American Revolution, signed the US Constitution, and is the namesake of Dickinson College in Carlisle, Pennsylvania, and Penn State University's Dickinson School of Law. He was also governor of both Delaware and Pennsylvania, a claim no other elected or appointed official can make. His home, Poplar Hall, outside of Dover, is open to the public as part of the John Dickinson Plantation, owned by the state.

- Before Lewes became a summer resort and beach town, it was home to menhaden fishing, an industry that kept men employed from Canada to South America. The fish swam here in the hundreds of thousands and were considered "the most important fish in the sea" by author H. Bruce Franklin. They were processed for oil, fertilizer, and an excellent food fish (for humans and livestock). Lewes was among the top fishing ports in the country because of the number of menhaden processed through the area. By 1966, they had been overfished to the extent that the local industry ceased to exist and processing plants closed. The loss of the menhaden has been detrimental to the waterways, estuaries, and up and down the ocean and bay food chain.

- Dover Air Force Base is home to the C-5 and C-5A Galaxy and is the largest military mortuary in the Department of Defense, serving as the entry point and mortuary for American military personnel and some US government employees who die overseas.

- The current state license plate design was first used in 1959, making it the longest-running design in the country's history.

- Delaware is the only state that doesn't have commercial airline service. If you want to fly in or out of here, particularly on an international flight, you have to go to Baltimore-Washington International Thurgood Marshall Airport (BWI) or Philadelphia International Airport (PHL). Scheduled domestic air service is also available at the Salisbury-Ocean City Wicomico Regional Airport (SBY) outside of Salisbury, Maryland.

- The Methodist Church of America was organized east of Frederica at Barratt's Chapel in 1784.

- The eleven concrete observation towers along the coast between Fenwick Island and Cape Henlopen were constructed between 1939 and 1942 as a World War II defense against German U-boat attacks. They were equipped so soldiers could spot and triangulate the location of enemy ships. They were not equipped with armaments. They ranged in height from thirty-nine to seventy-five feet and the walls were one foot thick. Two others were built near Cape May, New Jersey. Tower seven, in Cape Henlopen State Park, has been renovated and is open for tours.

- The Battle of Cooch's Bridge, September 3, 1777, was the only battle of the Revolutionary War that was fought in Delaware.

- Rehoboth Beach was the home of the country's first beauty contest, Miss United States, in 1880, with inventor Thomas Edison as one of the three judges.

- The St. Georges Bridge over the Chesapeake and Delaware Canal was damaged in 1939 when a barge ran into (it happened seven other times prior to the 1960 widening and deepening). The bridge was repaired and reopened in 1941 and designated for closure in 1995 until the Corps of Engineers decided it was essential to local traffic. The bridge was reconfigured in 2010 to allow for two bike lanes, making it the only bridge in the state open for bicycle traffic.

- Thomas McKean and George Read, two signers of the Declaration of Independence, were from New Castle.

- Woodburn, the governor's mansion, was built circa 1798 and purchased by the state in 1965. It joined the National Register of Historic Places in 1972.

- The earliest covered bridge seems to have been built over the Brandywine River in 1820–21. At the most, Delaware had about three dozen of them, almost all in northern New Castle County. Only two historic covered bridges remain, along with four newer covered bridges.

- As the US Constitution was debated and then approved in late 1787, the Delaware General Assembly offered land within the New Castle area to serve as the new country's capital. Of course, Washington DC was selected, but for a brief moment in time, there was a thought that the capital would be in Delaware.

- The Cape Henlopen Lighthouse guided sailors to safety during the night and through blustery storms from 1767 until April 13, 1926. Built by the British government, it was the sixth light constructed in America, and for a long time it was the second oldest light on the East Coast. The British were almost successful in destroying it during the American Revolution and again during the War of 1812. However, it was the inexorable determination of the tides that ate away at the ground beneath the light that eventually caused the light's demise. The light was removed in 1824 to the Cape Henlopen Beacon before the original light fell into the Atlantic Ocean.

• Francis V. du Pont (1894–1962), of the nearly ubiquitous du Pont family, was chairman of the Highway Commission from 1925 until 1949, during which time he supervised the design and construction of the Delaware Memorial Bridge, which opened in 1951. It was dedicated to those who died in World War II. The second span was added in 1968. When the original span was built, it was the sixth largest suspension bridge in the world. With the addition of the second span, it became the largest twin suspension bridge in the world.

• One week before his assassination, President John F. Kennedy attended the opening ceremonies of the Delaware Turnpike on November 15, 1963.

• Pierre S. du Pont built eighty-nine schools for black students between 1919 and 1938, some of which are still standing and in use through historical preservation programs.

• The Jewish Agricultural (and Industrial Aid) Society, formed in New York in 1900 by Baron Maurice de Hirsch, a German Jewish philanthropist, provided loans and training to immigrants who fled Russia and settled in Delaware between 1912 and 1929. Isaac and Ida Beinoff were Delaware's first Jewish farmers, settling in Kent County in 1897.

• The citizens of Delaware were divided during the Civil War, with most of the residents of Kent and Sussex Counties siding with the Confederacy. However, more than twelve thousand troops from Delaware joined the Union Army while only a few hundred joined the Confederate military service.

- The Selective Service was enacted in September 1940; it called for all men between the ages of twenty-one and thirty-six to register for the military draft. A month later, on October 16, 1940, registration started in Delaware and 35,215 registered. Eventually, approximately thirty thousand men and women from Delaware served in World War II. Delaware was involved on many levels, particularly because Dover Air Force Base, New Castle Army Air Base, Fort du Pont, Fort Miles, and Edgemore Coast Guard Base were within its borders.

- More than a century after the Civil War, with our country at war with Vietnam, the Veterans of Foreign Wars felt the Students for a Democratic Society (SDS) at the University of Delaware should not receive funding or a permit as an active organization on campus. The students prevailed as the university decided that they were constitutionally formed and could exist as long as they didn't break any rules.

- The whipping post or pillory was used to punish people found guilty of various crimes, although by 1889 it was against the law to discipline women in this manner. By the turn of the twentieth century, it was pretty much out of practice throughout the country. However, a man found guilty of wife-beating was flogged in public in Delaware 1952. By 1972 the Delaware criminal code prohibited the practice.

- Blue Laws (or Sabbath or Sunday Laws), which prohibited any type of secular activity on Sunday, started making their way into the legal code during the seventeenth century, ostensibly to promote moral conduct. Commercialism has whittled away at them over the years. In 1939, Wilmington residents submitted a petition to Governor Richard Cann McMullen to allow movies to be shown on Sunday after 2 p.m.

- During the Depression, the federal government created the Civilian Conservation Corps to countermeasure the high unemployment of youth. Camps were set up in Lewes, Magnolia, Leipsic, Georgetown, Slaughter Beach, Frederica, and Wyoming. One main function was to dig drainage ditches for mosquito control. The CCC also planted trees and built picnic, camping, and rest areas still in use today.

- When a JCPenney store (number 1,252) opened in Milford on October 11, 1929 (a little more than two weeks before the stock market crash of October 29, 1929), the department store had locations in each of the forty-eight states in the country.

- For years, starting in 1884, Lewes was a quarantine station for 200,000 incoming immigrants. As a ship entered Delaware waters, a doctor would check for such illnesses as yellow fever, cholera, smallpox, and typhus as part of the National Quarantine System. Those who were deemed to be sick or having been in contact with someone who was sick would be detained at the Delaware Breakwater Quarantine Station. It was also called the Delaware Breakwater Quarantine Hospital or the Marine Hospital and would eventually become a Navy base during World War I and then the fishing pier of Cape Henlopen State Park. Once the ship was cleared, it would continue to the port of Philadelphia.

- The Delaware Memorial Bridge, connecting Delaware to New Jersey, is named in honor of those who died in World War II, the Korean War, the Vietnam War, and the Gulf War. A memorial is located on the Delaware side, with other statuary, that lists the names of about fifteen thousand men and women from

Delaware and New Jersey. Ceremonies are held on Memorial Day and Veterans Day to honor their sacrifices.

- The Nanticoke River, starting in southern Kent County, is the only river in Delaware that empties into the Chesapeake Bay.

BIBLIOGRAPHY

"About the Brandywine Valley." www.thebrandywine.com/about/index.html.

Allen, Ken. "Grow Sweet Potatoes—Even in the North." *Mother Earth News Magazine,* June/July 2011. www.motherearthnews.com/print-article.aspx?id=2147495722.

"Amalgam (dentistry)." http://en.wikipedia.org/w/index.php?title=Amalgam_(dentistry)&oldid=480355297.

Amodio, Aimee. "Cape May Lewes Ferry." www.VisitNJShore.com.

Aston, Adam. "The War Over Offshore Wind Is Almost Over." *Bloomberg Businessweek,* June 26, 2008.

———. "Wind Energy Can Create Jobs, Reduce Carbon Footprint." *The Fiscal Times,* September 25, 2010.

Barnes, Eric. "Radiologists Prepare for Growing CT Role in Virtual autopsy." AuntMinnie.com, May 22, 2006.

———. "Virtual autopsy promises better data on US military casualties." AuntMinnie.com, August 3, 2006.

Bellows, Alan. "Outer Space Exposure." www.damninteresting.com/outer-space-exposure.

Black Jr., Lewis S. "Why Corporations Choose Delaware." Delaware Department of State, Division of Corporations, 2007.

"Cape May-Lewes Ferry." www.capemaylewesferry.com.

"Cases: 1960-1969 Term." *Burton v. Wilmington Parking Authority.* www.oyez.org/cases/1960-1969/1960/1960_164.

"Chesapeake & Delaware Canal." www.nap.usace.army.mil/cd.

"Chesapeake and Delaware Canal (C&D Canal)." www.pennways .com/CD_Canal.html.

"Conestoga Wagon." http://en.wikipedia.org/wiki/Conestoga_ wagon.

Cornwell, Patricia. *Port Mortuary.* New York: Putnam, 2010.

"Delaware Census State Data Center." www.stateplanning.delaware .gov/census_data_center.

"Delaware: Conflict in a Border State." http://americanhistory .si.edu/brown/history/4-five/delaware-1.html.

"Delaware Geology." http://delaware.gov/facts/geolog.shtml.

"Delaware Government." http://delaware.gov/facts/gov.shtml.

"Delaware Miscellaneous Symbols." http://delaware.gov/facts/misc .shtml.

Delaware Poultry Industry, Inc. www.dpichicken.org.

Delaware Scenic and Historic Highway Nomination Application, Harriet Tubman Underground Railroad Byway.

"Delaware State Animals." http://delaware.gov/facts/animal.shtml.

"Delaware State Insects." http://delaware.gov/facts/insect.shtml.

"Delaware State Plants." http://delaware.gov/facts/plant.shtml.

Diehl, James. *Remembering Sussex County (DE): From Zwaanendael to King Chicken.* Charleston, South Carolina: History Press, 2009.

"DuPont Heritage Timeline." http://www2.dupont.com/Phoenix_
Heritage/en_US/1939_c_detail.html.

DuPont Highway. www.aaroads.com/delaware/us-013.htm.

DuPont Highway. www.hsd.org/DHE/DHE_where_tranport_
Rt13.htm.

Ellison, Katherine. "Gone with the wind." Salon.com. www.salon
.com/news/feature/2007/03/28/wind/print.html.

Evans, Oliver, and Cadwallader Evans. *The Young Mill-Wright and
Miller's Guide.* Florence, Italy: Nabu Press, 2010.

Factsheet: Air Force Mortuary Affairs. Port Mortuary, August 2009.

Fichter, Jack. "Cape May-Lewes Ferry Puts Second Boat Up for
Sale." *Cape May County Herald,* July 22, 2010.

———. "DRBA Seeks Buyer for MV *Cape May.*" *Cape May
County Herald,* September 11, 2007.

———. "Could Ferries Evacuate Residents Before a Hurricane."
Cape May County Herald, September 14, 2009.

———. "Ferry: Not Just Transportation, a Destination." *Cape May
County Herald,* November 18, 2011.

Frank, Bill. "Arden: From Theory to Practice." *Sunday News
Journal,* Wilmington, Delaware, August 31, 1986.

Freudenrich, PhD, Craig. "Project Apollo Space Suit." http://
science.howstuffworks.com/space-suit.htm.

Francis, William and Michael C. Hahn. *The Du Pont Highway.*
Charleston, South Carolina: Arcadia Publishing, 2009.

"Garden State Parkway." http://en.wikipedia.org/wiki/Garden_
state_parkway.

George, Pam. "The Perfect Storm." *Delaware Today,* May 18,
2007.

Goldberg, Lawrence G., and Lawrence J. White. *The Deregulation of the Banking and Securities Industries.* Frederick, Maryland: Beard Books, 2003.

Grayson, William C. *Delaware's Ghost Towers.* West Conshohocken, Pennsylvania: Infinity Publishing, 2008.

"Grid Plan: Early United States." http://en.wikipedia.org/wiki/Street_grid#Early_United_States.

Handley, Susannah. *Nylon: The Story of a Fashion Revolution.* Baltimore: Johns Hopkins University Press, 2000.

Historian, United States Postal Service. "What's in a (Post Office) Name?" August 2008.

"The History of Nylon." www.caimateriali.org/index.php?id=32.

"Howard Pyle." http://en.wikipedia.org/wiki/Howard_Pyle.

Kane, Darren. *Glory Days at Delaware, Completely Unofficial Modern History of College Life in Newark, DE, UD 1987-2007.* Lincoln, Nebraska: iUniverse, Inc., 2007.

Knott, Joyce. *Plains, Kansas—100 Years.* Meade, Kansas, 1985.

Kotowski, Bob, and Nicholas L. Cerchio III. *Pie in the Sky: The Authorized History of Punkin Chunkin'.* Wilmington, Delaware: Cedar Tree Books, 2008.

Lewis, Emanuel Raymond, and Emmanuel R. Lewis. *Seacoast Fortifications of the United States: An Introductory History.* Annapolis, Maryland: US Naval Institute Press, 1993.

Lilley, Meredith Blaydes, Jeremy Firestone, and Willett Kempton. "The Effect of Wind Power Installations on Coastal Tourism." *Energies,* January 8, 2010.

Markovetz, Jessie. "The Balloon Floats into History." *The Review,* November 21, 2006.

McBride, David C. *Financial Center Development Act: Birth of a Banking Bonanza.* Wilmington, Delaware: Delaware Bar Foundation, 1982.

McCartney, Robert. "Wind Power Is Worth the Investment of $2 a Month for Maryland Households." The *Washington Post,* February 25, 2012.

McGovern, Terrance, Bolling Smith, and Peter Bull. *American Coastal Defenses 1885–1950.* Frating Green, Colchester, Essex, United Kingdom: Osprey Publishing, 2006.

Michaud, Christin. "Memories of 9/11 Resonate with Dover Port Mortuary Staff, Air Force Mortuary Affairs Operation," Official website of the US Air Force, 9/11/2011.

Miller, J. L., and Maureen Milford. "The First Modern Highway." The *News Journal,* August 8, 1999.

Miller, William J. *A Ferry Tale: Crossing the Delaware on the Cape May-Lewes Ferry.* Wilmington, Delaware: Delapeake Publishing Company, 1984.

Morgan, Michael. *Rehoboth Beach: A History of Surf & Sand.* Charleston, South Carolina: History Press, 2009.

Motavalli, Jim. "In a Blackout, Nissan, Mitsubishi and Toyota E.V.'s Could Function as Generators." The *New York Times,* September 1, 2011.

Murray, Molly, and Dan Shortridge. "Storm of '62 Still Making Waves." The *News Journal,* March 4, 2012.

"Oliver Evans." http://en.wikipedia.org/wiki/Oliver_Evans.

Quinn, Judith A., and Bernard L. Herman. "Sweet Potato Houses of Sussex County, Delaware, National Register Nomination." Center for Historic Architecture & Engineering, College of Urban Affairs & Public Policy, University of Delaware, January 1988.

Reese, Charles Lee. *The Horse on Rodney Square.* Wilmington, Delaware: News-Journal Company, 1977.

St. George's Bridge. www.nap.usace.army.mil/cd/sg.htm.

Salmon, James. "Cape May-Lewes Ferry as a Research Vessel?" Delaware River & Bay Authority, September 6, 2011.

Silicato, Dante. "American Dreams: Life in the Ardens." Examiner .com, September 9, 2011.

Smith, Chester M. Jr., and John L. Kay. *The Postal History of Maryland, the Delmarva Peninsula, and the District of Columbia: The Post Offices and First Postmasters from 1775 to 1984.* Burtonsville, Maryland: The Depot, 1984.

Smyrna Times, "Proposal for Tunnel under Delaware River." www.scsuntimes.com/lifestyle/x1273392873/75-years-ago-September-19-1935.

Stein, Mark. *How the States Got Their Shapes.* New York: Harper Paperbacks, 2009.

Stevenson, William "Bill" III. *Stone Balloon: The Early Years.* Wilmington, Delaware: Cedar Tree Books, 2005.

"Streptomycin." http://en.wikipedia.org/wiki/Streptomycin.

Svenvold, Mark. "Wind-Power Politics." The *New York Times,* September 12, 2008.

Sylvester, Phillip. "Sweet Potato Harvest, Curing, and Storage." http://kentagextension.blogspot.com/search/label/sweet%20 potatoes, September 15, 2008.

"T. Coleman du Pont." http://en.wikipedia.org/wiki/T._Coleman_ du_Pont.

2010 Annual Report. Delaware Division of Corporations.

Urban, Richard, Nicholas L. Cerchio III, and Paul Driscoll. *The City that Launched a Thousand Ships: Shipbuilding in Wilmington 1644–1997.* Wilmington, Delaware: Cedar Tree Books, 1999.

"US Route 13 in Delaware." http://en.wikipedia.org/wiki/US_ Route_13_in_Delaware.

Vinyard Shipbuilding, Milford, DE, www.shipbuildinghistory.com/ history/shipyards/5small/inactive/vinyard.htm.

Wheeler, Tim. "Study Sees Wind Energy Bounty off MD's Coast." *Baltimore Sun,* January 23, 2012.

Wray, Dr. Gary, and Lee Jennings. *Fort Miles (DE): Images of America.* Charleston, South Carolina: Arcadia Publishing, 2006.

Wroten Jr., Dr. William H. "Delmarvan Once Disputed Gen. Washington's Rank." http://nabbhistory.salisbury.edu/resources/ wroten/wroten_jdagworthy.html.

INDEX

ABOUT THE AUTHOR

Judy Colbert is a native Washingtonian (DC, not the state) who has traveled the mid-Atlantic area extensively since childhood.

"I went on school field trips as I was growing up, and then I was the 'room mother' for my daughters' field trips," she says. "All the teachers knew they could call on me to chaperone, regardless of which class it was. Okay, I did tire of the bread bakery and the potato chip factory and, for a while, even the zoo. On the other hand, when I traveled to France, I saw French rugrats sitting in the Hall of Mirrors in Versailles. When I returned home, I saw American rugrats doing the same thing in the United States capitol. Sightseeing with my granddaughters lets me enjoy the life and loves through still another generation's eyes.

"One great thing (among many) about living in this area is *everyone* comes to visit and that means I go sightseeing with my friends and family. I can always find something new or different and I love that much of my writing involves taking off and exploring. I'm naturally curious and I've always thought that I've been given a great opportunity enjoying that curiosity. When I'm driving, I am never lost although I may do some sightseeing that wasn't on my original itinerary."

A natural-born storyteller who has honed her craft for many years, Judy likes to wander into restaurants, libraries, and even beauty parlors to listen to the locals as they tell her to "Go talk to Uncle

Fred. He invented the wooden leg." And she responds, "I don't know if that's true or they're pulling mine. It doesn't matter."

Judy is an award-winning writer and photographer who is the author of *Maryland and Delaware Off the Beaten Path* (Globe Pequot Press), *Virginia Off the Beaten Path* (Globe Pequot Press), *Insiders' Guide to Baltimore* (Globe Pequot Press), *Chesapeake Bay Crabs Cookbook, Country Towns of Maryland and Delaware, Fun Places to Go With Children in Washington, DC, Peaceful Places Washington, DC, It Happened in Maryland* (Globe Pequot Press), and the forthcoming *It Happened in Arkansas* (Globe Pequot Press). She has written hundreds, if not thousands, of articles that have appeared in international, national, regional, and local publications and websites, including FreeFunGuides.com, *Recreation News,* and *Southern Maryland This Is Living.*

After thoroughly exploring the mid-Atlantic, Judy would like to spend a year or two cruising or sailing the seven seas, exploring other parts of the world, preferably without having to go to too many airports. She is a member of the American Society of Authors and Journalists, Society of Professional Journalists, Screen Actors Guild, and American Federation of Television Arts and Sciences.

THE FOLLOWING IS EXCERPTED FROM:

It Happened In Maryland

(September 2012, Paperback, $14.95, 978-0-7627-6970-4)

INTRODUCTION

If you picked up this book, you probably already know that Maryland is a dynamic, unique state. What you may not know is some of its fascinating history. The nation's seventh state may be small in size, but its people and history are anything but minor. Many events and notable people over the state's nearly four hundred–year history have shaped the country and even the world.

For example, techniques that dramatically changed the way we treat battlefield injuries to this day—and that have saved thousands of lives—were first implemented in Maryland during the Civil War. The predecessor to the nation's current interstate highway system originated in the state—in the 1800s, long before automobiles. And the state played an integral part in the Underground Railroad, Prohibition, and even the civil rights movement.

One piece of history that originated in Maryland has affected almost every American citizen, and is particularly dear to me. It all began with small, seemingly harmless turtles . . .

Prior to the 1970s, you could buy a cute little turtle for a dime or a quarter at a circus or a five-and-dime store. While I was a legislative aide to Prince George's County Councilman Francis B. Francois in the 1970s, these little critters came to my attention. They had earned a horrible reputation, as they were bred in human waste and subsequently were spreading salmonella. The dangers were obvious: salmonella can be fatal to infants and senior citizens, and can wreak scatological havoc on your household pet if it drinks any of the water in the turtle bowl. The hazards were too many, so the sale of these turtles could not continue.

After extensive research and documentation, Frank took up my turtle-ban mission and submitted a bill that would prohibit their sale within the county boundaries. It was adopted, and on the day the bill was signed, I was presented with a turtle pull toy. I was, from then on, officially dubbed the "turtle lady." My young daughters tried to buy a turtle at the local pet store to celebrate (or test) the bill's enactment, and they were told that some lady in Upper Marlboro had made it impossible for him to sell them.

Whenever someone felt the need or desire to give me a gift, it was a little turtle. I treasured these mementos made of china, wood, clay, seashells, cloth, silver, and a dizzying array of other materials. I finally stopped counting when my collection reached a hundred.

Within four years of the passing of the turtle bill, the federal government made the ban effective nationwide. The prohibition that started in Prince George's County made ripples throughout the nation. This event, along with countless other things small and large, makes Maryland so very one-of-a-kind.

UNDERGROUND RAILROAD

1835

Should you explore the nineteenth-century phenomenon known as the Underground Railroad, you'll run into lots of stories, most of them anecdotal and perhaps some debatable. The Underground Railroad started in its prime in 1831. It was neither underground nor a railroad that ran on tracks. Travel happened at night and everything involved was a secret (ergo, the term "underground," as was later used by spies during World War II) association of brave people, both white and black, who helped slaves escape from the Southern states. The people who led them from place to place were called conductors or engineers. The places where they stopped for food, shelter, and clothing were called stations, and those who owned the homes or businesses were station masters. Those escaping were called passengers, cargo, or goods.

Proof of these actions often is hard to come by because many of the people involved in helping slaves escape to Delaware on their way to the free North and Canada were compartmentalized. All they knew was who contacted them and whom they contacted. Helping to free slaves or even helping freed slaves travel north was a crime. So, for the same reason, few notes or records were kept. As any fan of police procedural books, television shows, and movies and of real life knows, you can't follow a paper trail if it isn't there. Fortunately, some notes and diaries were kept, particularly by people north of the Mason-Dixon Line, where slavery was illegal, so we can begin to understand what they went through and why. Runaway and freed slaves headed to Canada in particular, because slavery had been abolished there in 1834.

From this time and place comes the story of Harriet Tubman. Born a slave in 1822 in Bucktown, near Cambridge, Harriet committed her first reported act of defiance in the area where the Bucktown Village Store is located, sometime around 1835. She was helping a slave to freedom when she was hit in the head by the slave owner, which led to lifelong health problems and seizures. As a teenager she was hired out to John T. Stewart, who owned several farms, a shipyard, and other businesses. While there she met and married a freed slave, John Tubman, in 1844. Bucktown is where Tubman most likely learned the secret codes black mariners used and learned about safe places to live in the North.

Tubman escaped on September 17, 1849, and returned to help others escape. Making thirteen trips over the next decade, she helped an estimated seventy slaves—family members and friends—reach freedom. Providing assistance along the way were Jacob, Arthur, and Hannah Leverton (white Quakers whose brick home was known to be a major stopover), Daniel Hubbard (a free black ship carpenter), James Webb (whose log cabin can be seen on the 125-mile Underground Railroad trail), and Hugh Hazlett (who was captured and held in the Caroline County Courthouse in Denton for helping with the Railroad).

Samuel Green, a free black farmer and Methodist preacher, also was suspected of helping runaways. He was sentenced to ten years in prison at the Dorchester County Courthouse in Cambridge because he owned a copy of *Uncle Tom's Cabin,* the antislavery book written by Harriet Beecher Stowe in 1852. The courthouse that sits at 206 High Street was built in 1854, replacing the one that burned in 1852.

In addition to the people who ensured slaves' passage on the Railroad, some say songs helped to signal danger or a safe conduit. Such songs and spirituals as "Steal Away" and "Follow the Drinking Gourd" supposedly explained travel plans. The "drinking gourd" referred to the stars on the bottom of the bowl of the Big Dipper constellation that point toward the North Star. Other references indicated the Railroad was the freedom train or the gospel train that would take them to the Promised Land, or freedom up north.

Quilt designs were another possible aid to slaves seeking freedom. Anecdotal information indicates that designs were incorporated that showed a safe home, direction, or route or provided food, much as hobos riding the rails during the Depression in the next century would signal a home that provided food or an opportunity to work for clothing, money, or a bed. According to quilt theorists, there were ten patterns sewn into quilts that could be placed on a fence or clothesline, or hanging from a tree branch, alone or in combination, meaning "be prepared," "leave tonight," or "stay put." Even if apocryphal, this account conveys the unity and fear that all felt during the operation of the Railroad.

These slaves were fleeing owners who did not want them to learn to read or write, in no small part because they were afraid the slaves would read about escapes or learn to forge papers to prove someone was a free person. It's said that on one trip when Tubman was helping others escape, she pretended to be reading a newspaper and although people were looking for her, they knew she couldn't read, so they ignored her.

Many routes to freedom were land based, but others were via boats because of the proximity to the seventy-mile-long Choptank River, the Chesapeake Bay, and the Atlantic Ocean. Many boat or ship pilots were black and would hide fugitives on their way north. However, blacks worked as sailors, so it wasn't unusual to see them on a ship, even those captained or piloted by white men. Trains were used, too, and Frederick Douglass (1818–1895) was one slave who escaped by train from Baltimore to New York carrying freedom papers he borrowed from a black sailor.

Another incident involved John Bowley, a free black ship carpenter. His wife (Harriet Tubman's niece) and her two daughters were scheduled to be sold on the auction block in front of the Dorchester County Courthouse in 1850. The three of them managed to escape and Bowley spirited them away by boat to Baltimore. There they met with Tubman, who helped them reach safety in Philadelphia.

In 1854, around Christmas Day, Tubman led her three brothers to freedom from the area of Poplar Neck, Maryland. The property was owned by Dr. Anthony C. Thompson, who had many free and enslaved black laborers working for him, including Tubman's father, Ben Ross. Both her parents were also involved in the Underground Railroad and after her brothers' escape, Tubman feared for her parents' lives, so she returned to help them escape, too. As Tubman became better known, her life was ever more threatened and she had to abandon her trips in 1860. However, she did not retire quietly. Instead she continued her humanitarian practices as an activist, Civil War spy and nurse, and suffragist.

Assisting escaping slaves was a particularly brave thing to do in Maryland, where slavery had been legalized as early as 1660. When the Cambridge area of the Eastern Shore was settled in the mid-seventeenth century by whites from England, slaves, and free blacks, many were involved in farming. The original crop, tobacco, required many hours to grow and a lot of manpower—work done by slaves.

As the records are so sketchy, it's difficult to know how many slaves were escorted through the Eastern Shore and routes through western Maryland and other locales. It's difficult to know the effect of one person, such as Tubman, on the activities of others. A low estimate of escapees hinges around one thousand slaves a year from Maryland and other Southern states to a total of as many as 100,000 men, women, and children over the lifetime of the Railroad. Although the absolute numbers may have been small by comparison to the slave population, the psychological effect was enormous.

Finally, in 1864 slaves in Maryland were freed and the Thirteenth Amendment to the US Constitution abolished slavery. In 1865 the Civil War ended, with many of the events leading up to that point happening in Maryland's Dorchester and Caroline Counties.